*"I dedicate this book to Jargodin.
It was knowing him that inspired me
to write this book.
I can hear him chuckling to himself as
this goes to press."*

Front Cover: Jargodin wearing his ever present cap,
pictured with the author at Coober Pedy

All rights reserved. No part of this publication may
be reproduced, stored in a retrieval system, or
transmitted by any means, electronic, mechanical,
photocopying, recording or otherwise, without the
written permission of the publisher.

ISBN 0 646 21581 7

copyright ©

---JARGODIN---

The bewitching hour...A full moon flooded the silent semi-desert land of the opal capitol of the world----Coober Pedy. Mullock heaps from the opal mines looking like giant inverted icecream cones, stood as ghostly sentinels. Their white crumbled sandstone gave an eerie effect to the countryside.

Jargodin, his athletic body clad in dark clothing, stood in the dim shadows of one such heap. He blended in perfectly with the landscape. This was the Olympic field four miles west of the town; a field renowned for its superb quality of opal; a field which had produced untold fortunes. He stood motionless, in complete control, his eyes and ears alerted for any movement or sound. Little did he realise the impact his next hours work and following escapades would have on the small mining community.

Suspicion, hatred, fear and greed would replace mutual trust and camaraderie. Guns, intrigue, violence, and open defiance of law and order would take the place of peace of mind and open friendliness that had been the cornerstone of the mixed racial gathering of fortune seekers. Partners would begin to doubt each other___ miners on neighboring claims who had worked side by side for ages, would eye one another with suspicion. National hates and grievances, a carry-over from Europe, would surface.

Greeks, Italians, Hungarians, Germans, Jugoslavs and other ethnic races, found themselves retreating to the protection of ethnic cliques.

The herd instinct which the Australian way of life tended to ease, came strongly to the fore. The old religious hatreds of Moslems and Christians, which had lain dormant below the surface, would once again reveal it's dark side. The Jugoslavs more than any other group clung to their birth's identifications. They were either Serbians, Macedonians, Bosnians or Croatians. The animosity of wartime-- partisan----ustashia or otherwise, would surface...They became openly divided.

Jargodin made this an accepted way of life. His audacity knew no bounds. He started it...stirred it up...let it wash all around him... stole a fortune in opal and laughed. To the battler, who had struggled for years and had at last hit pay dirt, only to discover, that while he slept his precious opal had been taken from him, Jargodin was the 'Devil Incarnate.' He was hated, despised, admired and loved, but, you could not ignore the vibration of his presence....It had to be acknowledged...He became a folk hero and, to many and a legend.

He stared impassively at the winch some thirty metres to his front. It stood in clear relief of the moon's glow. There was the motor a metre and a half up the centre pole; The wire coiled around the drum then ran out over the steel arm to disappear into the darkness of the twenty metre shaft it bordered. All were directly in his view. He had stood there watching and listening....there was no one around...it was time to move.

He tensed...a nervous fear ran through his stomach. It was just like---like---like--- yes, he thought as a sense of exhiliration came over him. his thoughts raced back in time...images flashed through his mind...this is what I have been trained for...trained for...

CHAPTER TWO.

The nine year old boy standing in deep sawdust, stared up at his brother, 'Svonko the great,'....the star of the circus, as he swung on the trapeze in fluid majestic motion. It had been decided that he, Jargodin, could travel with the circus during school holidays. The owner and his wife, who were childless, had a large trailer and cared for him as their own. From the simple life of a peasant village in Bosnia Jugoslavia, which was still reeling from the aftermath of the war and communist control, the boy entered a dream world of magic. There were animals--clowns--acrobats--jugglers--but most of all, his brother....his God.

The lad could not be restrained. He wanted to be a star. It was a burning passion. He wanted to go direct to the trapeze and learn all there was to know. He wanted to be up there with his brother. His willingness to attempt anything, together with unbounding energy and pleading, penetrating, coal black eyes, soon had the artists preparing him for a circus life. It was as if, as the saying went, 'he was born under canvas'.

They taught him to tumble, to roll,

to climb, to fall, and, most important of all, to control his body through his mind. His capacity for work and training and his natural skill was amazing. It was heartbreak for the lad when the time came to return to the village for school periods.

Dolfo, Svonko's trainer, took the boy under his wing. "You must educate your mind," he would stress. "It all starts there." At first he was given simple isometric exercises as well as a routine to practise whilst back home. All of this was to develop strength and flexibility without retarding growth. At twelve he had his own spot in the circus. He did a slot routine of tumbles, somersaults and gymnastics that drew appreciative applause from the audience.

He was now fourteen. Dolfo would patiently explain each part of a sequence to him and, as if implanting his power into the lad, would hold his eyes in complete concentration quietly emphasising procedures. "You must imagine in your mind's eye over and over again, a picture of yourself doing every part of your exercise in perfect detail. Do it in your mind...not once...not twice, but a thousand times! Do it to perfection. Never settle for second best. If you do it up there," he would tap Jargodin's head, "you will do it on the night. It must be done in your brain first. Imagine it done to perfection. Imagine it, " he would stress through half clenched teeth as he thumped a closed fist into the palm of his other hand. Little did Jargodin realise he was being handed, by a revered trainer, the wisdom of ages and a secret to success of any undertaking.....persistent imagination....never had Dolfo such a devoted pupil. His body was developing into a perfect gymnasts build. He had progressed to the parallel bar, the horizontal bar and a complicated set of ground acrobatics. He did a three minute sequence with the aplomb and skill of an expert and received standing ovations...He was a star.

Some of the old hands watching his workouts marvelled at the ease and speed with which he would master new dimensions. They would shake their heads. Old Saldo would sigh, "ah, such brilliance, but such arrogance and impatience. The mixture is no good."

He lived only for the circus. The protection of the owner and his wife was of great advantage. They were proud of

their protege and to their credit they
made Jargodin learn English, as well as
developing his already acquired limited
knowledge of Italian and German. To them
the circus and its people belonged to
the world and they earnestly prayed and
believed the day would come when state
boundries would be of name only.
Jargodin was to be ever grateful for
their foresight.

Not all of them. however, showered
him with praise. Carlo, the animal
trainer would mutter, "Madre mio, that
one is no good. Those black eyes, just
like the devil." He would hurriedly
cross himself after such a statement.

The roar of the crowd and the
applause was food and drink to Jargodin.
He was good...He knew he was good.

Jargodin had just completed his act
and taken his final bow. The adrenilan
was flowing---his routine was flawless -
--his eyes glistened and his chest
swelled with pride. He skipped lightly
through the exit to the waiting Dolfo
who clapped him on the shoulder and
wrapped a cloak around his sweating
body.

"Well done. It was perfect. Tomorrow
we start on a new set of exercises---
more advanced. What do you say? You

think you are ready?" he smiled teasingly at his pupil knowing full well Jargodin's eagerness to do more and more.

Jargodin smiled back enthusiastically at his trainer. "Great," he said. "That's wonderful. Look, Dolfo, it's time for Svonko's act. I must watch. I will shower afterwards." Dolfo nodded understandingly as his pupil ran back into the edge of the arena. This was the ultimate act of the circus. His brother was to perform a double somersault, blindfolded before reaching the hands of the catcher. This was to be performed without the safety net. He stood there completely absorbed as his brother and the catcher went through the simple swinging warm-up exercises. The time had come.

Svonko stood on the landing high above the crowd. A blindfold was slipped over his eyes by the beautiful scantily clad Vanessa who acted as his second. Just prior the blindfold being placed on him, Svonko glanced down to where he knew Jargodin would be standing. The lighting made it impossible for him to see his brother, but he smiled as he raised his fingers to his forehead and gave a small salute. It was a ritual important to both. The announcement was made it echoed across the 'Big Top'.

"Ladies and gentlemen... Svonko the great... will... now blindfolded... do a double somersault... through the air... to the hands of his partner... master of the trapeze... Tullio!" Both men raised their hands in acknowledgement. The voice, pausing in the right places for effect and holding a steady far-reaching drone, continued. "The net has been taken away... We ask for your complete silence during this death-defying act!"... A hush fell over the crowd... all eyes were riveted on Svonko... wide eyed children, their mouths open stared in fascination.

The silence was broken by a steady roll of drums. Svonko left his stand, the catcher Tullio, doing likewise. They swung towards each other from both ends of the Big Top, back and forth..once..twice..three times.

The drums increased slightly in tempo and volume... NOW!!! Svonko left the safety of the bar.. Two quick somersaults completed, his outstretched hands seeking those of his counterpart.

The crowd watched in abject horror, gasping as one, as the hands of the catcher missed those of the artist. Svonko's highly trained reflexes knew immediately his fate, and in that split second his realisation of hoplessness was sensed by the crowd as he seemed to stretch his arms further, imploring and desperate, only to plummet to the ground dead in a twisted broken heap.

The crowd gasped in horror then screams and pandemonium broke out. Jargodin watched in agonising dread. He was first to reach his brother and stared in crazed disbelief at the twisted body before him. He became oblivious to everything. Turning he fled to the manager's trailer which held no secrets from him.

Going straight to a drawer he took out a revolver that was always kept loaded. He had been taught how to use the gun. Dashing back inside the tent he pushed his way through the circle of stricken circus hands. They stood stunned looking down at the body which had now been covered by a blanket. The catcher stood by, pale and trembling.

Jargodin shouldered up to him. "You bastard! You deliberately dropped him." Before anyone realised what was happening he shot Tullio at point blank range through the heart...Dead.

Police eventually restored order and cleared the crowd. A judge was procured and following an old time circus tradition, a court made up of circus people was held there and then inside the Big Top. Jargodin, his age taken into consideration, together with the tragic events, was sentenced to a reform school until he was sixteen, his case then to be reviewed...Never again was he to be allowed to work in a circus...Those riveting coal-black eyes lost all their shine to be replaced with a look of steely defiance against the world. ...His God was dead...they had killed his brother.

At reform school Jargodin became withdrawn. He continually worked out with isometric exercises and gymnastics. He became a loner. His eyes said, 'leave me alone.' At sixteen he was released and apprenticed in the magazine section of a mine in Croatia. As he grew into young manhood his body became strong and agile. By now he had taken to drinking large quantities of alcohol. Physically drink seemed to have little effect on him but, it freed his inhibitions and once again he became, 'the showman.'

To the delight of his drinking companions and to the amusements of customers, he would, for no apparent reason, perform somersaults or splits.

Many a quiet drinker would stare in astonishment as the person beside him would suddenly flip himself backwards in a somersault, do the splits, then doff his cap (which seemed ever set firmly on his head) in a theatrical bow. Usually the startled drinker, after recovering from his initial shock, would laugh uproariously and want to buy Jargodin a drink. There were occasions, however, when one of the more timorous types with mouth agape, would hastily quit the premises.

The mines, the small towns, together with post-war communist regime living conditions were not enough to hold him. His early years in the circus had spawned his dreams and desires to a life far outstripping the limited confines he now found himself. Through a series of off-colour adventures he escaped to Italy and, like many of his countrymen, found his way to Australia. After working in the mines in Western Australia for a period he headed to Adelaide.

Jargodin was restless and searching. In Adelaide he linked up with fellow Croatians and it was here he learnt of Coober Pedy.

CHAPTER THREE.

Jargodin shook his head clearing it of the images of the past to concentrate on the job in hand. The opal level was at sixteen metres. Looped in one hand was a twenty-five metre length of twelve millimetre diameter rope...long enough. A small pick was pushed through his belt and a four cell torch in an airline bag at his feet. Both hands were gloved...He was ready. Danger and apprehension sent a nervous thrill through his body. Aware of the penalty if caught, he banished all negative thoughts...He was here to win. Adrenalin coursed through his veins. "I'll show the bastards," he thought and grinned to himself. Here was his Big Top; the stars and moon his audience. He shuddered. 'Someone walked over my grave,' he muttered.

He picked up the airline bag and put the straps over his shoulder. He stepped out of the shadows and moved carefully over to the shaft...The career and legend of 'The Moonlighter,' was born.

Jargodin tied one end of the rope to the base of the winch pole...he tested the knot...safe. Expertly he monkeyed over the side and with practised ease he slid down the rope to the bottom of the shaft. Glancing up he could see a circle of stars high above. "Only you know," he laughed at them. He was both tense and exhilirated.

Taking the torch out of his bag, he switched it on and played it around. One short drive went to the left; neatly stacked against the wall were picks, shovels, a drill, buckets, fuses and the necessary odds and ends needed for a mining operation. On the floor of another drive veering off to the right were lengths of two inch galvanised pipe lying end to end. His torch followed their line to where they stopped just clear of the freshly blasted earth. During working hours the pipes were greased with sump oil; the fifty litre buckets would be filled with dirt, then easily slid along these pipes to the mouth of the shaft to be winched to the surface for dumping. This was the drive he wanted.

The drive was about two metres high, one and a half metres wide, and slightly narrower at the base. 'Good,' he mused, ' the opal level is at the top,' as he let the beam of the torch guide his way.

It was only twenty metres from the shaft to the work face. He stopped a few metres short and read the scene. The dynamited earth angled up to the face. The last blast had pulled about one and a half metres of dirt. A quick look showed it was well done. The ceiling of the blast was some thirty centimetres lower than the rest of the drive and the opal level. This thirty centimetres of dirt left behind would save the precious gem from injury. He sniffed the air... no fumes. There were other drives and shafts on the claim creating a good air flow, getting rid of any poisonous gases. Dynamite fumes could be lethal.

Tingling with anticipation he set to work. Holding the torch in one hand, with the other he wielded the pick with short quick strokes. He levered down the suspended level already weakened by the blast. He pulled down large loose chunks of rock, stepping back as they fell to earth. The pick sunk in and pushing the handle upwards he felt a large piece dislodge under pressure. A crisp crackling sound rewarded him...it was music to a miner's ear...opal...His heart beat faster...more pressure...more crackling...a large chunk was almost free.

He placed the torch safely on top of the rubble. Palm upwards he put one hand under the loose piece of sandstone taking the weight and with his pick he crackled the slab free.

He dropped the pick and with both hands eased it towards the light, turning it over in the process. "Holy Mother of God," he breathed.

A seam of red crystal opal a little over a centimetre thick, danced, flashed and sparkled it's tantalising colours before his eyes. He stared fascinated. 'Unbelievable,' he whispered. He was filled with that rare sensation of discovery. Turning the chunk this way and that, the colours changed like magic with each movement. It's beauty held him in awe...it was incredible. For millions of years this opal had been buried, its splendour hidden and now it was in his grasp.

Shaking himself out of his trance, he let the reality of the situation take control. There would be time to gloat later. He set to with a will and soon had quite a pile stacked on a smoothed out section of rubble. Working quickly and methodically, ignoring the smaller pieces which fell to the side, well placed intrusions into the slabs with the pick freed the glittering gems. Full coloured pieces the size of a cigarette packet lay in his hands.

Resisting all temptation to stare, examine and drool, he filled the airline bag with the biggest and best chunks.

With his mind racing ahead as he worked, he realised there was olenty of room for improvement in his whole operation. Already he was thinking of next time. One necessity was a large piece of canvas to spread on the ground to catch the opal as it fell. It would hasten the proceedure and the loss would be minimal. This was top quality opal and would fetch a good price. He was tingling with excitement edged with fear.

Part of him said, 'let's get out of here.' Another voice urged him not to leave any behind. The desire to be safely away won. 'To hell with it, I have enough...Let's go.' Before he could change his mind he zipped the top of the bag and, torch and pick in hand, made his way back to the shaft. He tied the pick and the straps of the bag to the loose end of the rope; the torch he placed inside his shirt. 'Now to get out of here,' he thought.

Jargodin reached up and grasping the rope, took the pressure. A deep breath, a quick look at the beckoning stars above and he felt he was back in the circus again. With practised ease he was soon at the top.

He paused just below the surface – this was the danger point. Cautiously he pulled himself up and peered around – all clear. With one final effort he was up and over, his chest heaved with exertion.

Quickly but surely he pulled up the rope, the airline bag and pick were soon safely in his grasp. The bright moonlight lit his way between the workings and he wasted no time getting back to his car parked a kilometre away. He reached his vehicle and placed his bag, torch, rope and pick on the floor behind the drivere's seat. He covered them with an old blanket.

He got in behind the steering wheel and fumbled in the glove box for cigarettes and matches. His hands were trembling as he went to light his cigarette. 'Take it easy, take it easy, 'he told himself. 'Take a few deep breaths.' He did as he commanded himself finding the tension that had held him together, abating and being replaced with exhiliration. He drew deeply on his cigarette and looked at his watch. Two hours since he had left.

Calmly he fired the motor. Once again the old discipline came to the fore. Beware of over confidence...Temptation to use his lights and flee was strong but had to be resisted. Driving slowly, he used the light of the moon as he carefully steered his way out of the field. He was soon on one of the many spider tracks that led on to a larger track and then the main exit.

He breathed a sigh of relief and switched on his lights...He was safe. He chuckled to himself. 'Can you imagine their faces when they go down there in the morning,' he thought gleefully. He had selected the claim with care. It belonged to Marcus and Stefan; two Moslems. They had called him a mug lair con man one day in the hotel when he had obliged a few of the drinkers with a couple of back somersaults. He had overheard the remark and vowed they would pay. 'They paid tonight. That will teach the bastards,' he grinned. He wanted to tell the world so they could applaud, but, with regret he knew it was not possible.

Thoughts of opal and money tumbled through his brain with alarming speed. Travelling slowly, eyes seeking the smoothest ride over the cocorrugated dirt road, he glanced up at the rear vision and with alarm spotted a set of headlights fast approaching.

His thoughts raced. 'I couldn't be followed...impossible. How come I didn't see their headlights when I came on to the highway? There was a large bend on the main road not far back; maybe they had not reached that when I emerged. There was one answer...Flee!!!

With Grand Prix acceleration the car lunged forward. A cloud of dust billowed up behind and hung in the still night air. Shooting glances in the rear vision mirror showed the headlights fading into cloudy dimness. He kept the accelerator down leaving a thick dust trail through which it was impossible to follow. Reaching a few galvanised shacks on the outskirts of town, he skidded around the corner of an almost impossible to see track with which he was familiar. He then wound his way down a maze of tracks which took him to the part of town known as the flats. Speed was no longer necessary. He knew he was safe. Slowly he drove around the outskirts of town to his dugout. He pulled up and slumped over his wheel. 'Jeez,' he thought, 'was all that necessary.

As did the majority of people, he lived underground. Old and new mine workings going into the side of the escarpments were blasted, picked, widened, or extended to suit and in some cases, provided ultra-modern accomodation. Extreme climatic conditions plus isolation and scarcity of building materials made these dugouts cheap and practical. Their chief asset was the relief from the searing summer heat which reached as high as fifty degrees celsius. The dugouts only varied four degrees winter and summer, ranging from eighteen to twenty-two degrees. Jargodin had purchased one of these from a departing lucky miner. It was located on a low isolated hill which gave him the privacy he desired.

Under the influence of beer and people he was the showman and performer, but then he liked to retire to his own dreams and schemes away from it all. His dugout was well appointed. A thousand gallon tank on top of the hill provided his water needs with more than enough gravity pressure. It was kept full by carters who made their living by deliveries from the water-board to the small community. A thirty-two volt wind generator, (called free lights), created power for lights,, washing machine and iron. A kerosene refrigerator added to his luxury. With a septic system and porta-gas hot shower built outside his entrance, he was as comfortable as he wished. He demanded life come up to his expectations and refused to live as a second rate citizen as he had so often been forced to do so in the past.

Still riding high from his nights work he parked his car relieved to be home. Resisting all temptation to look at his opal, he buried it under a pile of rubble outside his door. The next step was to get rid of his shoes, a ritual to be followed religiously in all his escapades.

He changed his footwear and with the ones he had worn that night in hand he wandered out on to the flat below his dugout. Ten inch prospecting holes were

all over the area. His torch soon found
what he was looking for. After dropping
a couple of stones down to make sure it
was free of dirt and not clogged, his
shoes followed the stones. After all,
his footsteps were all he left behind in
the mine...different shoes were a must.
Feeling more at ease he made his way
back to the welcome sanctuary of his
abode.

Taking a stubby of beer from the
refrigerator, he sat at his all-purpose
kitchen table. He was too excited to
sleep. As the number of empty stubbies
grew he surveyed his domain. It
cocsisted of one large excavation five
metres wide and ten metres long. At the
end on the left hand side, a further
space, four metres deep and three metres
wide had been blasted out and trimmed.
This served as a bedroom which retained
a sense of privacy by a large curtain
strung across the opening.
    Simplicity governed the room. A
solid table and chairs, two cupboards, a
couch, a small porta-gas stove a sink
next to the stove set against the wall
with the luxury of the waste pipe
running outside to the lip of the
escarpment. With the thought of new

found wealth he fantasised of improvements to his humble abode. Reaction and alcohol eventually took over and staggering to his room he slept.

He awoke refreshed. A quick glance at his watch revealed it was eleven a.m. Lying back he reviewed the situation. He had planned it well he thought. Since arriving in Coober Pedy he had spent a few days here and there with different ones of the Croation fraternity, going down underground and working with them... lending a hand. He had watched, absorbed and learnt all he could. He had helped blast, muck out and had even helped lucky ones dig out opal. He had watched them clean, sort and class the precious gem and by now had a working knowledge of it all. He had come to a very bold conclusion.

Why go down and work your guts out on chance? Why not let the other idiots do all the work, take the risks, pay the expenses, and, when they find it, go down and collect a share. Most of them were only peasants anyway he reasoned. Riches would be wasted on them. The Moslems, Macedonians and Serbians, would be his target. They would pay. Hatred handed down through the centuries was deeply ingrained in his character.

Having decided on his 'modus operandi,' he needed a cover. As with other miners on the field, he would become a pillar basher. This term applied to those who went down abandoned mines and rechecked the levels. They would put in a few shots of gelegnite here and there, hoping opal lay behind the walls. A lot of mining was haphazard and even the most experienced miners had left behind fortunes.

Pillar bashing could be lucrative. Most miners worked in pairs. They were well equiped with a generator, drill and a long two inch pipe to cross the mouth of old shafts. The pipe would hold a set of light steel ladders each ten feet long, suspended from each other. they would set up quickly, go below, drill holes, blast and after the fumes cleared, check their work.

Jargodin worked alone with a pipe to bridge the mouth of the hole and his trusty rope. He scorned the use of ladders. He only required a torch, a hand held brace with a small auger, some plugs of gelegnite, detonators and fuse, and he was operational. He would go down old claims, in areas where people would see his arrival and be aware of his activity. Once down he would look around, drill a few holes for the hell of it, blast, and spend some time daydreaming. Amazingly to his surprise he occasionally scored small amounts of opal. He would joyfully surface, taking great delight in his ascendency by rope. He visited the various fields, Olympic, Zorba, The Eleven Mile, The Twelve Mile, The Seventeen Mile...all of them. He had cemented his cover..

CHAPTER 4.

Eagerly he bounced out of bed and brewed a cup of coffee...he was too excited to eat. Retrieving his opal he soaked it in a tub of water, then proceeded to carefully clean it as he had been shown. He handled the pieces lovingly and drooled as each chunk showed its own characteristic beauty. The clean opal now lay wet and glistening on a large towel spread over the table; all excess sandstone and dirt had been cleaned away. There were large pieces, small pieces and chips, all beautiful and tantalising.

Turning on a reading lamp set up on the table he focused its beam on the gems, illuminating still further their enchantment. He stared in awe at the opal. He picked up piece after piece studying each and gazing at the flow of beauty as they were turned this way and that. He was out of his depth as to value. He was not experienced enough for the final part...he needed help...Who...Of course. Josef!!!..

Josef had had a disagreement with his partners and was not working. Apart from his thorough knowledge of the game, he was tight lipped. He, like Jargodin, had come through the iron curtain and there were episodes in his life that remained a closed book. Josef was also a Croation and hated the Serbians and Muslims with the same intensity as himself.

Carefully, Jargodin wrapped his stolen rewards in a cloth and placed them in the cold, never used oven of his porta-gas stove. He looked at his watch. One o'clock.

Josef would be at the restaurant...Ruffoe's..He'd best get there before he had settled in for a drinking session, otherwise another day would be lost. He was impatient to feel the money in his hands. Quickly tidying the room, he switched off the light, locked the door and was soon driving down the dusty road to town.

Miners were already pouring back into town from the fields. The main fields extended in a strip for about thirty kilometres north and a few kilometres wide. They all lived in town and travelled to and fro daily. Very few worked after one or two o'clock. By three p.m. the fields would be deserted. Clouds of thick red dust, stirred by the returning vehicles, could be seen for miles on the road stretching to the seventeen mile field, as they sped back to the comfort of the hotel or their dwellings.

After pulling into a vacant space in front of the restaurant he entered the cool interior. The drawn curtains across the windows gave welcome relief from the harsh glare outside. Already the place was crowded and would remain so until the early hours of the morning. As his eyes adjusted to the soft lighting he spotted Josef sitting alone in his usual place in the far corner. He wound his way through the tables acknowledging various greetings with a nod of the head or a quick grin and the inevitable 'chiao piasano.'

Josef watched Jargodin as he made his way towards him. They had a lot in common and had drifted together becoming friends. 'He's a rare one,' Josef thought. 'He smiles and jokes but we still don't know anything about him. He never talks about himself. He's deep and I think, could be...deadly.'

As Jargodin neared his table he manouvered his foot and pushed back a chair opposite him, nodding to Jargodin to be seated. Jargodin grinned his thanks and pointed to Josef's near empty stubby. "Drink up piasano." He looked around and catching the eye of a waitress, pointed to the stubbie on the table and held up two fingers. She nodded. Jargodin turned back to his companion. "What's new mate? Still the gentleman of leisure?"

"Yeah, no hurry, anyhow the way I feel today, the last thing I want is to be down a bloody mine. I got tangled up with a mob of bloody Greeks last night. They're on opal and were letting their hair down. They didn't say much, they didn't have to, but from what I can gather they have hit it good out at the sixteen mile. Seems like every man and his dog are getting opal out there. Anyhow they just kept buying and buying. They wouldn't let me shout. I got as drunk as hell. Can you imagine me drinking with a mob of Greeks...I hate their guts." He grimaced. Jargodin laughed.

"What about you my friend? Any luck pillar bashing?" He watched Jargodin carefully.

"Yes, as a matter of fact, I have. That's why I came looking for you. I've got a bit of opal and," he paused, "I think it is pretty good. Can you give me a hand to weigh and class it?"

"When?"

"As soon as you like. I could do with the money." Josef thought for a while then looked around the room.

"Now if you like. Let's get out of this place. I could do with some fresh air. You got anything to eat and drink around at your place. I'll have to put something in my stomach and I'll need a few more stubbies to feel well." Just then the waitress arrived on the scene with two stubbies. Jargodin paid and tipped the girl.

"Okay, let's drink these and then we'll go. I have some beer back at the dugout and there is plenty of salami and cheese and odds and ends. Good enough?"

"No problem. I'll pick up my scales on the way."

Jargodin looked at his friend and chose his words carefully "I didn't realise you had little time for the Greeks."

"I worked with a team of them when I first arrived. I didn't have a clue and could barely speak the language and boy, they ripped me off as I later found out. Never again. They can't help themselves. When it comes to money, they would rob their own grandmother. You can't trust the bastards......I got square."

Those last few words spoke volumes to Jargodin. His mind was already thinking ahead. Josef could be handy. He looked at his friend with new eyes. Medium height, slim, but wiry. He was a fair haired Croation with a ready laugh always giving the impression of a quiet easy going, couldn't care less type of guy. Jargodin realised that he also was one who never talked about himself. 'Josef,' he thought, 'you and I could do business.'

CHAPTER FIVE.

Josef had the opal sorted into four small piles. The reading light was on and pulled low over the table. He took an occasional swig out of the stubbie of beer beside him. He would then run his fingers through one of the piles - hesitate - pick up a stone - reappraise it - then put it on another lot. Time and time again he repeated the process. Jargodin stood back, silent, watching, afraid to break Josef's concentration, and desperately curbing his own impatience. After what seemed an eternity, Josef stood up and stretched satisfied at last and nodded to the opal.

"Beautiful stuff. Bloody beautiful." He pointed to each gleaming pile in turn. "Tops, seconds, thirds, chips," he said.

Jargodin nodded concealing his excitement. How much was it worth? Five, ten thousand? Josef spoke. "Weigh each lot, then wet them and put them in these plastic bags." He pulled out a roll of plastic bags from his hip pocket. "Mark the weight on each bag.

Jargodin did as he was told. The opal now wet once again, took on a fresh glistening radiance. 'This is how it will look when it is cut and polished,' he thought. The bags lay before him. "What do you think, Josef?"

Josef frowned in thought, peering at the opal. "Good gear for sure. The tops should be worth $2,000 an ounce...the seconds $1,000 an ounce...the thirds, $400 anounce, and the chips, $50 an ounce."

"Jeez," exclaimed Jargodin. He had been writing the figures down and now tallied it up. He looked at his friend and grinned. $25,000 ! Holy bloody hell! Madre Mio! It's unbelievable!"

Josef smiled back. "Yeah, a nice little parcel" He emptied his stubbie. "come on, mate, give me anóther drink and something to eat before I die of starvation."

Jargodin busied himself. He was jubilant but showed no emotion. '$25,000,' he thought, 'for two hours work.' He chuckled to himself. They sat eating salami and cheese and drinking beer. Josef gestured towards the opal. "Pillar bashing is a good business eh? Where did you get it?"

The question took Jargodin by

surprise as you normally don't ask those sort of questions. He hesitated....Josef held up his hand and shook his head. "Hold it amigo. I don't want to know. I should not have asked. Good luck to you. Let's hope there is plenty more where this came from."

Jargodin smiled back. "No worries. It's no great secret. I got it out at the twelve mile," he answered evasively.

Josef paused, a stubbie half way to his mouth. He looked at his friend then burst into laughter. He chuckled to himself and shook his head slowly side to side. "Jargodin" he laughed, "I told you, I don't want to know, but, my friend," he pointed to the opal, "That opal came from the Olympic field."

Jargodin paled. What had happened. Impossible...nothing went wrong. He recovered his thoughts quickly. "What makes you say that?"

"When you have been here as long as I have, you can tell. Each of the fields have their own characteristics. Anybody with experience can tell which opal comes from what field."

Jargodin had had a fright, but had just received a valuable lesson. "I've a lot to learn." He shook his head.

Josef smiled. "Don't worry. I wont

be following you to find your valuable claim, but, if there is any more of this stuff out there, I would advise you to peg it straight away and make it legal."

"No, it's worked out. I was just lucky to strike this small pocket that had been missed. It's not worth while following."

"Okay then. What do you want to do with this stuff? Do you want to sell?"

"Sure as hell I want to sell."

"Okay, let's go. You want me to sell or would you prefer to do it yourself?"

"No, no. You do the talking. I'll just look, listen and learn."

"Alright. We will ask $30,000 and maybe settle for $23,000. What do you say?"

Jargodin just nodded. It sounded unbelievable.

They drove back into town. "Go to the hotel," Josef said. "McLean is here from Andamooka. He's a good buyer and pays well. He always stays at the pub. Bugger the Chinese...they want to cut you down to nothing."

McLean sat at a small table in the hotel room. The door was open. He looked up and watched the two men approach. He beckoned them inside pointing to two chairs. "How are you boys? You have some opal? He nodded to the bag in Josef's hand.

"Sure, Mr. McLean. Olympic. Top quality."

"Good." McLean smiled and extended his hand. "You're Josef. We have done business before."

"That's right. This is my partner, Jargodin." He inclined his head towards Jargodin who sat beside him.

McLean looked at Jargodin and once again put out his hand in greeting. He had been a buyer for years and had developed a poker face that gave nothing away. "Gawd," he thought, as he returned the firm grip. 'Where did this bastard come from. It's like looking into a black bottomless pit. He's dangerous this one.'

Jargodin, a half smile on his lips as he acknowledged the greeting could sense McLeans unease. "Nice to meet you Jargodin. Let's hope we can do some good business, now and in the future."

"I am sure we will Mr. Mclean,"Jargodin smiled back.

'Hell, the bloody smile never left his mouth,' McLean thought.

"Right boys, let's see what you have." Josef placed the opal on the small table. McLean switched on the reading lamp adjusting the flexible arm to bring the shade to the centre of the table at eye level. He opened the various packets sliding the contents onto the surface. He was thorough, holding pieces up to his eyes with the 100 watt bulb in the background. The two men watched silently as the buyer concentrated.

McLean looked up at the men. "How much?"

"$30,000," Josef replied.

McLean raised his eyebrows and turned back to the parcel giving it another appraisal. He sat back with a sigh. "It's good opal...that I won't deny, but $30,000 is too much. $25,000 is the best I can do."

Josef looked at Jargodin...Jargodin shrugged his shoulders as to say, 'whatever you think.'

Josef turned to McLean. "How about an extra grand Mr. Mclean? Make it $26,000."

"McLean laughed and shook his head. "Okay Josef. You drive a hard bargain. $26,000 it is."

McLean bent down to a briefcas4e on the floor beside him and extracted bundles of $50 bills all banded together in lots of $5,000. He pushed five of them across to the men, then pulled out another two $500 lots from another bundle. "26.000. Count it."

"No need," Josef shook his haed. They shook hands all around. The deal was over.

McLean looked at Jargodin who was watching the money. He could have sworn his eyes changed lustre, like a car changing into overdrive. 'This is a rare one,' he thought.

Jargodin looked at the buyer and smiled. "We will do business again." He stated it as fact.

McLean nodded. 'You're a confident bastard,' he thought. 'there is something I don't know here...and don't want to know.'

They sat on opposite sides of the table in the dug-out, the money on the table before them, each a stubbie in hand. Jargodin counted out $2,600 and put it before Josef. Josef pushed the money back. "I did it as a friend."

"Listen amico, I could not have done it without you. You earnt every cent of it; besides I'll need your help in the future. Ten per cent is a going rate. Let's keep it on a business basis, because I need your expertise." He pushed the money back. "I insist."

Josef shrugged and took the money in his hands. "Okay...Thanks." Josef looked at his watch. "You're too late for the bank, my friend. You had best hide it somewhere. Are you coming down for a few drinks."

Jargodin had been looking at the money before him. $23,400. The most money he had ever seen in his life, let alone being able to call it his. He felt good, he was on a high...this was just the start. Josef's voice brought him back to the present. He knew what he was going to do.

"Josef, I know by your standards and the big money that is being made, this is not much, but, to me it's a bloody fortune and just the start. Ever since I have been here, I have seen guys strike it rich and over night become week-end millionaires. They have strutted around, big time, the centre of attraction down at the card games and all the rest of that bull-shit. A couple of weeks later, they're broke. Not for me. I've got things to do and it doesn't include playing Manila with those card sharps. I need a time away by myself. I'm off to Adelaide for a couple of weeks. I need a better car and a few things. I'm going to hit the trail now. I'll throw a few things in the car and head off. It will be mainly night travelling and will be a lot cooler."

"Good thinking paisano. Get down there and live it up for a couple of weeks. Book in to a motel and sample the night life. Be careful if you go to the Croation club. There are guys who hang around there just waiting for guys like you coming down from the opal field with money in their pockets."

"Yeah, I know what you mean but I'm one jump ahead of those bastards," he laughed. "Josef," his tone now serious, "I need a gun. Do you know anyone down there who may be able to help me get one."

"Shit, you can get a gun up at Beppe's here. He's got shot guns, twenty-twos, 3-0-3's, whatever you want."

"No...not that type of gun, I want a pistol, a revolver."

Josef raised his eyebrows. "Jeez....I...don' know." He paused. "Look I've a very good mate down there who may be able to help. He runs a card game in a broken down section of town, but don't be fooled by that. He's a big business man in his own right and has all sorts of influence from the police down to the hoods of the town. He's got his finger on the pulse on everything that goes. He's a Croation and as Australian as a meat pie. You wont find him at the club. He keeps away from all that racial bullshit. He's happily married with a wonderful family. His wife is an Australian girl. He has been out here for years. He' straight, and,..tough. You don't do the wrong thing by him," Josef stressed. The two men locked eyes in understanding. Jargodin nodded.

"I don't hand his name or telephone number out as blokes have gone down from here with big heaps of money in their pockets and gone around to him asking all sorts of favours. They think because he came from Croatia like them he was going to fall over backwards and welcome them with open arms. 'Josef,' he said to me, ' these peasants come down here loaded, full of their hates and grievances from the old country and because they've got money in their pockets, they think are big time. They are still ignorant bloody peasants, the scum of Jugoslavia that Tito kicked out of the place. He was happy to see them go. They come down lording it about but it isn't long before the three G's, girls, grog and gambling send them back again to their picks and shovels, poorer, but unfortunately no wiser. Keep the bastards away from me.' They're Johnnies words. Anyhow," he reached across and picked up the pen and paper from where it was left when they tallied up their opal before. "Here is his name and phone number give him a ring. Tell him I sent you."

Jargodin, his spirits high, eagerly headed for Adelaide, anxious for what the big city had to offer.

CHAPTER...6

Adelaide, capitol city of South Australia, with its wide streets and beautiful parklands, was a welcome relief from the hot, dry, dusty, semi-desert regions of Coober Pedy. Jargodin had been busy since he had arrived. He had booked into a motel in Greenhill road and was enjoying the luxury of his accomodation as well as the restaurants of the city. He had traded his old 1966 model Holden in on a 1970 station wagon and had it thoroughly overhauled. He had deposited $10,000 with the bank of New South Wales in King William street which gave him a sense of releif as well as security.

Clothes were another part of his agenda . He liked to be smartly dressed and his athletic body only enhanced the clothes he wore. He outfitted himself with a new wardrobe down to socks and underware. He never wore a hat, but, among his purchases were two new dark checkered caps. These details out of the way, he rang the number Josef had given him and made arrangements to meet Josef's friend, Johnny Dandovic at eleven a.m. next day.

The phone rang...a waiting hand picked it up. "You calling Coober Pedy 725135," the operator's voice asked? " Your number is waiting. Go ahead please."

"Thank you...hello...Nick?"

"Yeah. Nick speaking."

"Dandovic here Nick. Johnny Dandovic."

"Hey Johnny, good to hear your voice. How are you? How is things in Adelaide?"

"Good paisano. What about you up there? You still robbing the opal miners in that pigsty you call a restaurant?"

Nick laughed. "Now, now, Johnny...you know me. I give them what they want...good food..cold drinks, and cheap prices with pretty girls serving on the tables."

"Bullshit Nick," Johnny humoured back. "Your prices are okay because you know they will pull the bloody place down if they're not. Your food is lousy because they are a mob of peasants that eat there and they wouldn't know any better. How the health department hasn't closed you down, I don't know, but, let's face it, there is no health department up there. As to the pretty girls, what a joke...Bloody painted young prostitutes that have been run out of Adelaide..Strictly third class amateurs. You wont give them a job unless you can lay them in that back room of yours. How your not poxed up, I'll never know. Anyhow I want a favour."

"Yeah, I know." Nick was chuckling at Johnnies description of his establishment which they both knew was virtually spot on the truth. "You only ring me when you want a favour. What is it?"

"Josef...Josef Mazurin. I need him to ring me. Can you get a message to him?"

"Yes, sure Johnny. He comes in all the time as a matter of fact, I think he is here now. Hang on Johnny, I'll check."

"Hello, hello, Johnny? This is Josef. What's the matter?"

"Nothing Josef. How have you been? Everything okay?"

"Sure Johnny. Sure. What is the problem?"

"No problem Josef, it is just that I got a phone call from a guy called Jargodin. He wants to see me. He said you recommended he get in touch. I thought I'd check. Do you know him?"

"Yes, sure Johnny. No worries. I gave him your number. You know I wouldn't give your number to anyone. He's okay. Comes from Bosnia. I've had a lot to do with him. He's deep, doesn't talk about himself..He's okay."

"Ah, that's good Josef. I thought I'd check. As long as he is not one of those radical Moslems, or pro or anti Tito fanatics. I can do without them coming around claiming life long friendship just because they come from the old country. Half the basrards would cut their next door neighbours throat for a dollar."

Josef laughed. "I know what you mean. No this guy is not interested in politics or religion. He was christened a Catholic he was telling me, but that is as far as it goes. No problems Johnny."

"Good Josef. You had better come down soon and pay us a visit my friend."

"Will do Johnny. My regards to the family. Ciao."

"Ciao, paisano."

The taxi pulled up at an old run down two storey building at a dead end of an equally dead end street in Port Adelaide. The driver pointed. "There it is...prosperous looking joint isn't it?

They must be saving it for the next Alfred Hitchcock movie."

Jargodin eyed the place, nodding his head and agreeing with the driver. "Tell me," he said, "do you ever get much work of a night to places like this?"

The driver, a middle aged friendly Australian spoke. "It's amazing, I do a fair bit of night work and this place is always good for jobs throughout the night. Not many, but a few. The first time you come down here, you feel like turning around and going for your life, but, we've never had any trouble from that joint." He nodded at the building. "Some sort of card game goes on there I believe. I don't know, and," he stressed with a laugh, "I don't want to know. I've plicked up the owner a few times...Johnny...Nice guy, but, I wouldn't want to cross him. He must, however, run a clean joint otherwise the police would have closed him down ages ago."

Jargodin eyed the place as the driver spoke. You want to know about a place, ask a taxi driver...they know. He absorbed it all as he looked at the buiding in front of him. An espresso bar long since out of business, with heavy draped curtains across the windows, stared back at him. There was a heavy chain and padlock on the door, that would do no more than keep out the poor unfortunates who roamed the area, looking for a place to sleep, protected from the elements. A door next to the espresso bar he had been told...if you weren't looking for it, you would miss it.. He paid the taxi with a decent tip and expressed his thanks.

'Phew!' Jargodin exhaled his breath..'some class,' he thought to himself. These sorts of places were familiar to him; he had survived through places much, much worse than this on his way to freedom.

Slowly he turned the door knob and eased the door back. A straight flight of stairs, dim and unviting, led up to a landing over which was suspended a pale light. He absorbed it all and slowly mounted the staircase...the steps creaked. A reasonably new handrail ran alongside the inside wall...using this to keep balance he stealthily ascended, placing his feet at the extreme sides of the wall...no noise. At the top of the landing and to the right was an open door. He quietly walked up to the door and looked around.

To the left a counter came out from the wall and arched around, creating a kitchen and servery...a dividing line from the rest of the room which contained a dozen tables and chairs to suit. On the counter of the servery was the inevitable espresso machine. A two door domestic refrigerator back against the wall, no doubt contained drinks and food items necessary for sandwiches. Popular brands of cigarettes rested on a sad looking shelf where packets of Bex powders were prominent.

Standing over a sink also against the wall a swarthy, muscular man, his sleeves turned back to the elbow was washing coffee cups. A pile of freshly washed ash trays lay upside down on one side of the sink.

Jargodin watched the man, taking in his clean shaven square slavic features, well groomed salt and pepper hair, the immaculate, persil white shirt..the chunky gold watch on his thick left forearm. The man had not heard him enter, but... he had 'felt' him. Looking up quickly he saw Jargodin's smiling face studying him.

The man looked at Jargodin, not revealing the quick feeling of apprehension he had felt. He didn't like to be crept up on.'This has to be Jargodin,' he thought. He looked into the smiling face and coal black eyes...eyes that seemed to dance with amusement. 'This is a rare bird this one.' His eyes gave a quick appraisal...about one hundred and seventy centimetres...athletic...fit...very fit..smart..he noticed the clothes, a cap worn at the hair line at a slight angle...a long sleeved expensive shirt buttoned at the wrist...This bastard could be dangerous...he's certainly different...interesting.'

Jargodin could almost hear his thoughts. The man grinned at him. "You must be Jargodin."

Jargodin nodded. "you are Johnny Dundavic. Josef speaks highly of you." By this Johnny had wiped his hands on a towel and put his hand out over the counter. The two men shook hands with a firm clasp.

"Coffee?" Johnny asked.

"Sure. Black no sugar, thanks."

"Sit down." Johnny nodded to a table. "I'll bring them over."

As often happens in life, two people meet and find an instant affinity and trust...and so it was. They each recognised in each other, something that set them apart from the common herd. Little things like gestures, poise, conversation, dress, but more importantly the eye contact. All these things seemed to set an approval on a person.

"They talked, probing and discovering links along their trails that gave a common bond. Both shared a good sense of humour and found themselves laughing at some of their antics in the old country as well as the embarassing mistakes made by all newcomers to the country.

"Okay, amico. You didn't come here to inquire after my health. What is it you want. Incidentally, it is Jargodin isn't it? No other name?

"Nope, just Jargodin." Johnny raised his eyebrows and shrugged.

Jargodin paused. He doesn't muck about..."Well it's like this, I want a revolver."

Johnny looked closely at him...."You know, you can go to the police and get a licence for a revolver...On the opal field this is no problem as most miners at times handle large amounts of cash."

Jargodin nodded but remained silent...

"If however, you have something to hide, they wouldn't issue one," Their eyes locked.

"Nothing to hide. I have a clean slate and want to stay that way, but, I want a revolver without anyone knowing."

"Johnny shrugged. The request was not unusual.

"That's not all. I want a machine gun."

Johnnies eyes opened wide. "Jesus, Mary, Joseph!!" he exploded then began to laugh. "What the fucking hell do you want with a machine-gun. You think you're Al Capone or something. You going to have another Valentine's day at Coober Pedy. Jesus!!" He got up from the table and went behind the servery. "A bit early for me, but I'm going to have a brandy, You want one?"

Jargodin laughed. "Sure, I'll join you."

Johnny was shaking his head. "Don't pull jokes like that on me mate."

"No joke. I want one."

"You're fair dinkum!" Jargodin nodded. "Look paisano. You seem like a guy that has a lot going for you. You don't need anything like that bullshit. There are enough idiots running around this country now as it is, and, I'm sorry to say, a lot of them are from our country, This is a great country and it doesn't need some television cowboy with a machine-gun to add to its troubles." He got up, took the empty glasses and walked back around into the servery. "I'm going to have another brandy. Do you want one or would you prefer a beer?"

"A beer would be fine."

Johnny took a sip of his drink and thoughtfully looked at Jargodin who was quietly sipping the stubbie before him. "Look, a pistol, yes, no problems...can do. Lots of guys want a pistol...Makes them feel good. Makes them feel they're someone they aren't. They feel tough. Big guys. They see too much television. 'Some guys need one I can tell you...they have a real reason for one...without one, they could not sleep at night, but, a machine-gun, Madre Mio!! Means you could be crazy, and somehow I don't think you are. Therefore, what have we got? It means you are one... meam... very mean, dangerous guy.

'Now what happens? You're going to do something serious...soon. That means trouble...that means police. It is quite possible that both you and your machine gun are in the hands of the police in a very short time. Naturally they will want to know where you got the machine-gun... They are funny that way. Let's say they are inquisitive people." He gave a wry grin.

"Jargodin, my friend, no matter how tough you might be, they are tougher. They would soon have you telling them where the gun came from... believe me. Then what happens? The axe falls on me... Bang! I am washed up... look around." He waved his arm around the room... "A dump... illegal card games and booze to the players if they want it... They let me operate; they know what goes on here and could close me up tomorrow. They're not fools. I'll tell you why they let me operate... the cards are clean and there is no trouble here. Anyone getting out of line here is out... period. They don't come back. No drugs allowed here. No prostitution. Sure, some of the girls come up here and spend a bit of time. They know they can come here and relax, have a yarn, drink some coffee or beer. They know they will not be molested or troubled. Some of them are girl friends of the guys who play.

'Most of the people who come here

are gamblers of the true sense of the word. You would be surprised at some of our clientele. Anyone who has had a lucky night can leave when they choose to...We ring a taxi if necessary...Nobody is allowed to leave for at least ten minutes after they have gone. Sometimes, in the early hours of the morning the police arrive and drink coffee. Nobody takes any notice of them. Sometimes I help them, providing it doesn't interfere with my own moral code." He leant back in his chair. "Capise?" Jargodin nodded.

They sat silent for a while the older man studying this adventurer before him...he intrigued him. He did not know what it was, but he could sense destiny in this guy, and, he was afraid he might be involved. He was not a gangster of the stereo type, of that he was certain...what was it then?

Jargodin sat silent and waited. He knew Johnny would help...somehow.

Johnny nodded at his empty stubbie. "Another?"

"Yes, I wouldn't mind, thanks."

"I'll have one also." Johnny got up, got the stubbies and came back. They sat and sipped.

"I'll tell you what I'll do. You

tell me where you are staying. I will get in touch with someone. They may be able to help. A parcel will be delivered to you and you give them the money. You will not know where it came from or the person who delivers it...okay?

Jargodin thought for awhile. "Okay, the only thing is I won't let you know where I am staying until the morning I leave. I want to get away on Monday morning...three days time. I'll ring you and you can get in touch with them and I'll wait for the parcel. How's that?"

Johnny thought it over. "Fair enough." AT least The bastard's smart.

"How much will it cost me?"

"$2,000, all told."

"Deal." He extended his hand. They shook hands and the deal was sealed.

"Phew," Johnny said. "I hope you don't come to town too often," if you're still alive , he thought.

They both heard the noise at the same time. Someone was running up the stairs. Both their gazes went to the door.

"I'm out of condition," she said as she stopped in the doorway. Jargodin was captivated by the girl standing a few yards away. His computer like brain registered the facts with lightning speed. About 160 centimetres...dark curly hair nestling around a face of milk white skin enhanced by a pair of dancing brown eyes... a perfect set of smiling white teeth. Her chest was rising and falling with the exertion of running up the stairs, revealing well rounded breasts, struggling to free themselves from the confines of the top that held them in restraint. A gold cross and chain hung from her neck, the cross snug between the swelling of her breasts...a tight pair of jeans showed off the well moulded curves of her hips and legs... A pair of gold sandals added to the vision before him.

Jargodin looked at the girl and for that split second their eyes locked. That undefinable split second look, that has happened untold times throughout history and will continue to do so: that split second that has more power than all the words or gestures; that split second of 'Fate,' that will not be denied: that split second that gives that feeling of knowing; knowing that this was and is inevitable; of somehow just knowing. Paula with that woman's intuition handed down through the ages knew.... Jargodin knew.

CHAPTER 7.

Johnnies face lit up as he rose from his chair. He took her outstretched hands and gave her a peck on the cheek. "Paula! Lovely to see you. What are you doing? June only said to me this morning that she was going to ring you about coming out on Sunday. We're having a bar-b-que. The usual thing you know. The kids haven't seen you for what now?" he laughed, "must be two whole weeks."

She joined in his laughter conscious of Jargodin, now standing , watching her closely.

She was aware of her confusion. Her first re-action was like that of a startled fawn...that would flee to safety, but, once there, would turn and timorously return, one step at a time, drawn to the inevitable... Who was he?...Was he one of Johnnies patrons?...She felt his impact.

"Paula, this is Jargodin. He is down from Coober Pedy for a few days. Jargodin - Paula," and by way of explanation, 'Paula is an adopted daughter into our family. Come, Paula, sit down. Would you like a coffee or a soft drink, or,' he pointed to the stubbies, 'something stronger?'

'A coffee would be lovely, thanks, Johnny.' Her original intention was to give a message to Johnny and continue on her way, but now... What now?... Like a moth drawn to a flame, she must wait and see what happens. She was excited, but, a voice kept saying, 'don't be stupid. He's just some guy passing through,.. yet...'

They made small talk. Johnny kept the conversation going, unaware Paula was much quieter than normal. Jargodin was hoping that each bit of conversation would reveal more about her. He had to see her again. Johnny hadn't mentioned her surname. Where does she live? Where does she work? Does she work? She spoke perfect English, but she was of European extraction... of this he was certain. Italian? South Italy? Maybe. He couldn't be pointed in his desire to see her again as Johnny would have had a heart attack... this he knew for certain... Fate, however, was running the show.

'Well, children, as much as I would like to sit here and talk, I am afraid, I must prepare for the night's entertainment.'

'Yes, I must away also,' Paula said.

Jargodin saw his chance. 'I too, have to get back to town. Could you by chance drop me off somewhere close to town, or near a taxi rank please?' He looked at Paula.

With more calm that she felt, she answered. 'Certainly. I'm going into the city. It will be no trouble at all." Johnnies protective instinct over Paula didn't like the idea of her being in Jargodin's company, even for a short trip to the city, but what could he say without appearing ridiculous? With a feeling of unease he said goodbye to both telling himself not to be 'bloody stupid'. The saloon bar lounge had the new look now prevalent in so many hotels across the country. Modern decor, soft lighting, aiming for an atmosphere of class, intimacy and privacy, far from the macho image of the beer swilling institutions of Australian drinking habits.

It was now fashionable to be seen, although discreetly, at these venues. Office girls rubbed shoulders with company directors, while matrons gossiped at a table in the corner.

Tall, well-groomed, wearing excessive fashion jewellry, the girl serving in the island bar handled the customers unobtrusively with the skill of long experience. As Jargodin breasted the counter, her eyebrows raised in question to him. He was equally vocal and pointed to a seven ounce glass along the bar, indicating the size, then raised one finger. She nodded. He took his drink over to a wall. There were a few vacant stools and a shelf along the wall for glasses. He sat on a stool and took a sip of his beer. 'Would she come? Please God...hold it you bastard..who are you to call on God?...well please...please come.

She said she would...she wasn't having me on...was she?...His mind went back to the trip into town; a pleasant drive along the wide streets; the awareness and excitement of that intangible electricity between them. Expertly she had pulled into a vacant parking space in King William street. She looked across and smiled at him. 'How's this?'

'Fine,' he answered. 'Look please do not get me wrong, but ....oh hell...please, I am only down here for a short time. I'm staying at a motel in Greenhill road and in truth, I'm a complete stranger in town. I'm not married or anything like that and I would dearly love to take you out tonight." He spoke quietly but earnestly, his eyes held hers in his plea. He reached over and gently took her near hand off the steering wheel and brought her fingers up to his lips. His gaze never shifting, "please?" he asked.

A slight blush came to her cheeks. She wanted so much to know this dark-eyed stranger who had so suddenly came into her life. She was scared...scared of herself and the feelings this encounter had aroused in her...Don't run away Paula, a little voice whispered..It seemed an eternity before she answered.. She nodded her head slowly. "Alright," she whispered. "I'll meet you at six O'clock in the lounge at that hotel." She nodded to a hotel across the road. Jargodin barely heard her words but his heart responded.

"Wonderful," he said squeezing her hand. His face lit up as he smiled in relief.

He looked at his gold Seiko watch that, in a moment of happines, he bought after leaving Paula. 'You're early . It's only ten to now. Jeez, your behaving like a bloody school kid. Let's face, she's out of your class. All your life you have only knocked around with peasants and the scum of society'.....His mind flashed back..'Thank God, for the manager and his wife of the circus who had instilled in him manners and a want for better things. Who told him always to seek the best.. Thanks to one of the teachers at the reform school, who had led him into the secrets of books for self education, a habit he had retained. At least, he could conduct himself with decorum, and, was well read...hadn't they always told him, never settle for second best...Oh shit, who are you trying to kid...you should be down the waterfront in some dive, doing somersaults off the bar and throwing money around in some drunken orgy...'   "I'll give you a penny for them."

He swung around. "Paula!" He smiled with embarassment. "Please forgive me ," he laughed. "I was miles away. I have been watching out for you, but just for the moment, I had turned around and...."

"You seemed so deep in thought and so serious, I didn't like to break in," she smiled back at him. He looked at her. She was dressed in a simple black dress that showed her figure to perfection. With just a trace of make-up and a slight touch of lipstick, her skin glowed with health.

"Let me look at you. You are beautiful." His eyes went heavenward in mock thanksgiving. "What have I done dear God, to deserve such an honour."

She laughed. "Well, I guess, that line is different."
The ice was broken. They were two people attracted to each other. The the night was before them.

CHAPTER 8

They moved to a secluded table in the corner. Jargodin got the drinks; a bacardi and coke in a long glass for Paula and a beer for himself. She took a sip of her drink and nodded in appreciation. "Tell me, is Jargodin your first name?"

He smiled. "No, but that is what I am called and it suits me fine.'

She looked into his eyes. This guy is certainly different. Caution signals went up; this was no ordinary encounter; somehow she felt that here was a situation she might not be able to control or, she thought with a trace of panic, might not want to control.

Both could sense a current between them. They jockeyed light conversation back and forth. They skirted the reality of the situation as they eased into each other's personalities. They moved closer to each other with slight intimate gestures, then withdrew, leaving an avenue of retreat without bruising. This was not what she had expected. What had she expected? As they talked they found it easy to converse. They found laughter, over simple little things, came readily and naturally. With mutual consent they went to a chinese restaurant . Unbeknown to each other, they had both, by now, accepted the, 'che sera, sera, attitude.

At the rstaurant they leisurely ate through various small courses. The food, although excellent and enjoyed, mattered little to them. It was a time killer as they probed, advanced and retreated in a game as old as time...The courting game. Jargodin wanted this woman more than anything he had ever wanted in his life. She knew her decision time was not far off; she knew he wanted to sleep with her but kept pushing the reality of the situation into the background. Both drank little, neither wanting alcohol to be decision maker.

They couldn't sit there much longer. Patrons had come and gone. They were lingering over their second cup of coffee. The table had been cleared of all traces of their meal. Jargodin looked at his watch. "It's ten thirty," he said quietly.

They both fell silent, each knowing that one ill-timed or mis-placed word could break that tender emotional thread. He was afraid she would run...she was afraid he would say something that would rob her of the subtle dignity allowing her to blend in with the inevitable.

Paula was both excited and apprehensive. Fate had dealt her a deck of cards. She decided to play her hand.

He leant forward over the table and taking both her hands in his, his eyes softened. He spoke softly and earnestly. "More than anything in the whole world, I want you to come back to the motel with me. I've wanted you from the moment I set eyes on you. I can't afford the luxury of time of getting to know you. Please."

She steadily gazed into those coal black eyes that seemed to penetrate to the bottom of her soul. She made that womanly decision made innumerable times before her. She nodded. "Let's go," she whispered.

Naked, her hands clasped behind her head, she lay stretched out on the bed looking at the ceiling. Holy Mother? she asked herself. Is this really me? Did this really happen, knowing full well it had and had been so different from anything she had ever imagined and twice as wonderful. She felt complete for the first time in her life. She felt as if she had thrown away the cloak of uncertainty and doubt.

It was the complete giving and discovering of each other, culminating in complete unity of body and soul. She was in love...hopelessly so and she accepted the fact. She turned and looked at the sleeping body beside her. "You bastard," she whispered endearingly, "I still know nothing about you, but you're mine and who the hell knows what it will bring." She curled up beside him and slept.

CHAPTER. 9.

"So there you have it all," he said. He was reclining on the bed, a couple of pillows under his back, proping him up against the bed-stead. It was pleasantly warm in the room...a stubbie, cigarettes and ash tray were on the small bedside table within reach, She, her breasts bare and wearing only a small pair of vees, was lying back in a similar position on the opposite bed. She had remained silent throughout, intently watching this attractive, athletic, complex character to whom she knew she was now totally bound.

Eventually she spoke. "That explains a few things...Jargodin...not John Jargodin, or Charlie Jargodin....just Jargodin. Like Zorba, or Zorro, or Houdini....There may be others with the same name, but, there is only one Jargodin....the one who always wore a cap...The cap...now I understand...all the circus people wore caps..it was an important part of your past." She spoke slowly. "It has been the one thing you have had to cling to ...to hold of your past. Maria Mio."

She got up from the bed. "I need another cup of coffee." She filled the small electric jug supplied by the motel then set up two cups adding the contents of the small packet of Nescafe to each one. "You certainly are one big surprise."

Jargodin watched her as she moved around the unit. 'My God, she is beautiful.' A twinge of conscience floated across his mind as to his recent escapade in Coober Pedy also the figure of Johnny Dondovic kept appearing before his eyes. How was he going to handle it all? He pushed it into the background. Like Paula, his heart was ruling his head and for the next couple of days he would let nothing interfere with this new found bliss. They had awakened early marvelling in the fact of them being together and had made love. They had showered, breakfasted and Jargodin had informed reception, that his wife had arrived so his bill was to be adjusted accordingly. They revelled in discovering each other.

The coffee made, she brought the cups over to their bedsides. Quietly she spoke. "I have the feeling there are many more surprises in store for me." She held his gaze. "I also have the feeling that this was meant to be. We have just met, but, I am in love with you. You see, I know these things. There is that grass roots peasant in me. I have this strong intuition bred in me that has been the difference of survival or death in our family for generations. You have been honest with me, I will try to do the same."

She lit a cigarette and settled back on the bed. With a far away look in her eyes she spoke. "I'll make it as brief as I can, you will have to read between the lines. I was born in Sicily and came out to Australia when I was four years old: born into a very strict Sicilian family in the true sense of the word. We went to Ingham in North Queensland as we had relations there...many relations, not, only by breeding, but by blood...Mafia blood. We were a big family...Cosa Nostra, Mafia, Black Hand Gang, Omerta, call it what you like, but, the people concerned refer to it as, 'The Family.' It was and is, very strong...You'd be surprised."

She looked steadily at him, but, he gave no re-action. She continued.

"As has been the case for generations, It was taken for granted as to who I would marry. A marriage of convenience, a marriage that would strengthen the ties of two very powerful families...Johnny La Motta...that was the poor bastard's name...Well, I grew up like any normal girl until I was about eleven years of age, then the chaperoning started. Parental control became more evident. I was good at school and wanted to go to University and study chemistry...I'm getting a bit ahead of myself.

"Sundays, of course, was a standard ritual. Firstly, church; you had to go to church...the older women always severe in black, the men in their suits, and the children in their Sunday best. The boys would have their hair slicked down with brylcreem; the girls with pink ribbons in their hair. Oh God, the same old thing, Sunday after Sunday and the services seemed never ending.

After church, would be the visiting; the chicken and spaghetti; the wine; the women all yabbering together; the young kids running around screaming; the older ones awkward in their good clothes constantly being watched from sly angles by mothers and aunts. How bloody awful.

The La Mottoas were always at our place, or we were at theirs. I did not like all this and of course would object. As far as I was concerned I was an Australian and wanted to go to the beach, or down the river swimming with some of my school friends. As I got to the fourteen and fifteen mark, the reins tightened, The tighter they got the more I rebelled. I had a good ally in my brother, Bruno; he was older and had grown into a typical Australian; we often made fun of 'the old way,' as we called it. My mother couldn't speak English and refused to learn...It used to make Bruno and I ropeable, She was always talking about ,'how you did things in the old country'...the bloody old country,

Dad was fluent in writing as well as speech. He had been out in Australia before we arrived. I often talked about going to University and every time the subject came up, it was side-tracked, or, 'let's wait and see how your exams turn out.'

I was seventeen when the bombshell fell! I was to marry Johnny La Motta!!!...I was stunned...I thought it was a joke, but it was no joke...I couldn't believe it...we were living in Australia, not, Sicily. They couldn't do this to me!!!...I nearly went out of my mind..I was hysterical. They had to get a doctor to give me a sedative...naturally, a doctor of Sicilian descent...one who would understand. I refused to leave my room...I wouldn't eat. I just lay there not wanting to believe this was happening to me. They were selling me, a prize bloody virgin.

"They were all worried. Bruno was furious. He would come into my room at night and try to get me to eat something. He did not know what to say...He understood,

One day they got the priest around...Father Russo...another good Sicilian priest...He would talk some sense into me. Everybody in the district knew he was having an affair with a woman down the road whose husband had died a couple of years before,..It was common knowledge. You can't keep those things secret in a small community like ours, especially when he was seen leaving the farm at daybreak. His car was always there. Well....my mother knocked on the door this day.

"Paula, Paula," she called, "Here is the Father to see you." I didn't answer. She cautiously opened the door and poked her head around into my room. I was lying on my bed, sheet up around my neck, looking at her.

"Paula," she said sweetly. "Here is the Father". She nodded to the priest. "You go in Father...talk to her."

He closed the door when he came in. There was a chair beside my bed and this bastard just pulled it out and sat down.

"What seems to be the trouble my child? Ah, the pains of youth," he nodded condescendingly. "Yes it can be a very confusing period. A time when we think we know best, but, we would be better off if we followed the wise advice of our parents."

" I looked at this moon-faced, smooth skinned, slimy fraud, with his patronising smile...Well, I had had enough of being pushed around and this fake was the last resort. He wasn't much taller than me, but, round and plump.

She started to giggle as she relived the scene.

"Like all good Catholic families we had crucifixes or holy pictures in our rooms. I had a ststue of The Virgin Mary on my dresser. It was about thirty centimetres high and heavy...'Pray to the Holy Mother for advice....', I didn't let him finish.

"I leapt out of bed, picked up the statue and hit him over the head with it," she started to laugh. "He didn't know what happened....he went down on his knees...there was blood pouring out of his scalp,,'Get out! Get out!' I screamed. You sanctimonious bastard. You are screwing that bitch down the road and you come here telling me what to do, you slimy bastard. You only want my father's money. You've got all these bloody peasants shit-scared you're going to send them to hell you lousy fraud." She looked at Jargodin who sat, silently laughing with her, barely able to control himself.

"Well," she chuckled as she continued, "I had broken the statue over his head and still had the biggest piece in my hand. It had a pointed jagged end. The priest was bellowing like a stuck pig. He staggered to his feet and shoved the door open which knocked my mother, (who was listening on the other side), head over heels on to the floor. As he staggered out still screaming, holding his head, with blood pouring out through his fingers, I jammed the sharp end of the statue up his backside... Take that you bastard," I screamed at him. Paula was now laughing and holding on to her side. Jargodin was shaking his head from side to side trying hard to subdue his laughter.

Paula straightened up and with a few chuckles continued. "Talk about pandemonium!" Her eyes opened wide as she recalled the severity of it all. She started to laugh again.

"For God's sake," Jargodin managed to say . "Steady up. Jeez. Talk about a spiritual awakening...The priest crowned by the Virgin Mary."

Paula wiped tears of laughter from her eyes. "You know, I think it was the first time I ever really swore in my life. I shocked myself at what I had done. I realised then and there, scratch me and the peasant wildcat is there and I will fight tooth and nail for survival. It was the best thing that could have happened to me. I said, 'right you bastards, you're not going to beat me. I am not going to succumb to any of you. This is my life, Mafia or no Mafia.'

'All of a sudden I was hungry. All I can remember was the priest driving off with a blood-soaked towel around his head and my mother wailing aand running over to the neighbours.

'It was really on then. Not much later Bruno and my father came storming into the house. I had just eaten a mortedella sandwich and was enjoying a cup of coffee...In they came and just stood there. They are both big men, each over one hundred and eighty centimetres. Here they were, these giants just standing there looking at me. She giggled again. I looked up and said, 'what do you bastards want.' Well you should have seen the stunned look on my father. I'm sure he thought he was hearing things. Bruno couldn't help himself. He started to laugh. My mother started to wail...she had come in with them. My father must have wondered what the hell had gone wrong with his nice orderly household, and, was this his daughter speaking to him like this?

'My father turned to my mother and snarled, 'shut up.' She did. He glared at Bruno who was shaking his head and silently laughing. 'What the hell is going on here? What's this about you trying to kill the priest."

'Oh, Jesus, I got mad. I'll tell you what it is all about. This is not the old country and you're not going to stuff up my life with this Mafia shit. My father winced when I said this. Leave me alone or I'll kill myself and I'll probably kill that fucking putana priest as well. The bastard got struck by religion, I yelled . I hit him over the head with the statue of the Madonna and,...I jammed the jagged edge up his arse. Well....my mother's wails increased, Bruno fell up against the wall holding his stomach in silent laughter, I thought my father was going to have a heart attack...and, I continued, if you think I am going to marry that slimy, buck toothed, Sicilian slob of La Motta, your crazy. Anyhow with a bit of luck that priest of yours might die with loss of blood before he gets to hospital. I slammed down my coffee cup and stormed out. Just leave me alone. I mean it....

To say my parents were stunned would be putting it mildly. Never had I sworn or carried on like that. In a way, I think my father was proud of me that day. I think he saw something in me that, as a boy, he had seen in his family back in the old country when they had lived in poverty; before they had fought their way into respectability.

As I was leaving, my mother started to say something and my father turned to her and growled, 'leave her alone.'

"What to do with me? That was the big problem.

CHAPTER 10.

They left me alone and put out word that I had had a nervous breakdown due to too much study. This was the cover as the La Mottas were becoming inquisitive. Then they came up with the wonderful idea of sending me back to Sicily for a holiday, as I needed a rest. I welcomed the idea. Anything to get away. Bruno would come into my room of a night and we would talk. He was proud of me over the priest incident. 'Jesus,' he would say. 'I'd loved to have been there to see that.' Bruno was as Australian as could be. He played football, was in the Lifesaver's club and was a popular guy, not only with the guys. He was tall, dark and handsome, as the saying goes. He was the sort of guy that, if a war came, he would be the first to enlist to fight for Australia. He hated all this subterfuge but, he knew that 'Family,' was going to a big issue in his life with which, one day, he would have to contend. 'Hell sis,' he would say. 'We don't need to be involved in that Mafia rubbish. We are wealthy people and have the farm. We don't need anymore. We should tell them to get stuffed....we're out ! Finito.'

'He knew deep down , as I did, you could not say , 'chiao paisano. No more....we've had enough.' It didnt' work that way.

'I was welcomed in Sicily by my Aunt and Uncle and God knows how many 'Cuginas.' They came from everywhere to meet their Australian cousin. My Uncle was wealthy and I now became more aware of what we were as a family. I began to notice things I would not normally have done. It became more apparent of the extent, 'The Family,' had spread it's tentacles. Strangers, whom I never got to meet would arrive at all sorts of odd hours....conversations behind closed doors, lasting until all hours of the morning...well dressed, quietly spoken men, many with American accents, came and went.

CHAPTER. 11.

'Once I tried to talk to my Aunt about these people. She firmly told me, that it was none of our business. Our job was to run the house. We see nothing and hear nothing. End of conversation. Well, in a way, I was happy there and kept putting off my departure. I guess I was only postponing the inevitable. They would look at me in a funny way when I said, I wasn't sure when I would go home, but they never asked questions. Actually they liked having me there and didn't put any pressure on me.

'I stayed there fourteen months, sending home the occasional letter and postcard. I came back to Australia determined to leave home at the first oppurtunity. I knew I would have to plan it carefully.

'I arrived back to a new car as a welcome home present. This suited me fine. They gave me a bit of breathing space and I used it to advantage. I had quite a bit of money of my own which my father had deposited in my account. Altogether I had about $10,000....that with a new car, I could go anytime.

'Insinuations were being made that I

had had my fun and it was now time for me to grow up and honour my responsibilities.... that meant Johnny La Motta. He was becoming a real pest. Every chance he had he was over at our place, as he had been given the understanding we were to be married. Things were getting unbearable. Bruno tried to talk to my father, all to no avail. 'That is the way of The Family,' was the response. He would come and talk to me. 'What the hell are we going to do sis?' he would ask. I'd tell him not to worry that I would sort it out. The thought of that big sloppy creep fondling me made my skin crawl. In the last couple of weeks I was at least civil to him to allay any suspicion and to take attention away from myself. The family thought I had come to accept it.

'I had one close friend in town. We were cousins, and her father was a solicitor. They too, had been out here many years and although I am sure they were 'Family,' there was none of this marriage farce. The boys of the family carried the role and that was it, full stop... She knew my situation and was horrified. Her father had tried to reason with mine about it, but no way would father change his mind.

'Well, I needed her help which was willingly offered. I was to spend a weekend in town with them, but, unbeknown to my parents, her family would be away leaving Maria home alone. I had been in the habit of taking the odd garment into Maria's place and leaving it there, so together with a small overnight bag of a few personal things, it was all I had. It was enough - all I wanted to do was to get away as far and as fast as I could.

'I avoided Brisbane and Sydney and came across here to Adelaide. I rented a unit with a garage, put the car in there until the registration had run out and then re-registered it here. I kept in touch with Maria. I would send my letters to a friend of hers in Townsville and she would change the envelope and send them on,

All hell broke loose when I left. Maria told them I had told her, that I was going overseas. The hunt was on as I had broken a code of honour....It was a cardinal sin.

"After changing my name slightly, I went to night school and did a secretarial course. I have joined an agency and do part time work which suits me fine. It was a lonely life and the inevitable happened. I met a nice guy, we had a few drinks too many...he came back to the flat and I lost my virginity.' She shrugged as she looked at Jargodin. 'What a bloody disaster. We were not suited and I couldn't get rid of him quick enough...no electricity.

He kept coming around wanting to continue our relationship so I decided to move, which I did. There were two girls in that block that I became friendly with, and unbeknown to me they were prostitutes. God, I was naive. I didn't have a clue and we became friends...they were quite nice really. Anyhow one day down town I bumped into them. They were having a barbecue on the Saturday afternoon and asked me around.

'I had nothing better to do and so I went. It was there I met Johnny Dondovic. He had dropped in on his way home from the races. It was coming on towards dark and I decided it was time for me to leave. Johnny had come by taxi and when he found out I was going through the city, he asked me to drop him off at a taxi rank...MMM... sounds familiar.' She gave him a sly grin.

'I pulled up near a cab rank and there was an espresso bar nearby, so Johnny asked me if I would like a coffee. We went into the cafe and sat there and talked. He told me all about his family. I just told him I was from North Queensland and that I had gone to night school and was doing part-time work. He asked me how I came to know the girls, meaning the ones at the flat. I told him that I had once lived there and had run into Sylvia in town and she had invited me out. I told him the male traffic had got a bit heavy for me around there so I had moved out.

He laughed. 'Of course you know what they do for a living,' he said. 'I didn't know. When he told me, all I could do was blush. How dumb could I be. I looked at Johnny amazed. 'You don't think that I...I.....' This once again set him laughing. 'No, no, I could tell you wern't of the same...ah...calling, I was just interested to find out how you knew them. We often laugh over that.

'Well, Johnny must have felt sorry for me. He asked me to come out to their home the next day and meet his family. I went and fell in love with them immediately. His wife June, took me under her wing. His son and daughter, both teenagers, treated me as a sister.

'It was later that evening...other people had gone home...the children had disappeared...we were alone when I told them the full story. It was a great relief to me to be able to unburden myself. Both June and Johnny made it clear that their home was my home; June frets and worries over me; I take the kids out and, they take me out. We are always on the phone to each other...in fact I love them dearly.

'Oh, Jesus,' Jargodin thought. 'What about your family?' he asked.

'Oh, yes, they found me. The old saying, you can run, but you can't hide from them. It was a Sunday morning. I had been to church.' She shrugged. 'Old habits die hard. I was sitting there having a cup of coffee. I was going to Johnnies for lunch and was debating with myself as to whether I should go as I was, or change into something more casual. The doorbell rang...I wondered who it could be...I opened the door and there they were...my father and Bruno. My father brushed straight passed me into the flat and checked out all the rooms.

'Bruno just said, 'hi, sis,' and stood there with a silly grin on his face. He at least came forward and gave me a brotherly hug; I wont bore you with the dramatics.

'I rang June and told her what had happened. She got Johnnie on the phone and he insisted I bring them out. If I wasn't out there in the next twenty minutes, he was coming in.

'Well, I think they got one big surprise. Johnnies place is quite palatial, set in an acre of ground. When we arrived, there were families in their Sunday best, having been to church as I had. It was similar to our Sundays up home, the only difference was there was a mixture of Jugoslavs and Australians. Johnny, when dressed, is rather an impressive man and commands respect. I could see that my father was duly impressed.

'June and Johnny took control. Johnny introduced my father and Bruno around. In fact, my father actually enjoyed himself. He was among self-made men who had come up the hard way. At one stage, Johnny took my father inside with him and they did not emerge for over an hour. I don't know what was said, but they emerged friends.

'Bruno had time to fill me in on all the gossip. A rift had developed between the La Mottas and our family over my behaviour. Johnny La Motta had married another good Sicilian girl brought out from the old country. They had sold their farm and moved to Stanthorpe.

'After my family had wasted a lot of money on an overseas search they knew I was still in Australia...it was quite simple really, Bruno said. He didn't elaborate, They had known where I was for some time.

'You have won so far sis,' he said, 'but remember...you're being watched...you're still Family and some day...some day, you may have to pay the price...I sincerely hope not.'

'Anyhow, that is about it. I have been told, that I must go home shortly, behave and get married like a good little girl should.

Jargodin gave a low whistle. 'Where do we go from here.'

Paula stood up pulled off her vees, and lay down beside him. 'I know where you're going,' she said.

CHAPTER 12.

It was six p. m.... The heat of the day had eased. It was now warm and pleasant as they strolled over the soft green grass.

'This is absolutely crazy,' she laughed. 'Here we are walking hand in hand in a park over the road from the motel, just tyenty-four hours after meeting each other. You took me out, dined and wined me, took me back to your room, stripped me, and,' she gritted her teeth in mock severity, 'fucked me, and fucked me, and did all sorts of unimaginable things to me,' she threw her arms around his neck. 'I loved every minute of it and want more.'

He laughed. He disentangled himself and did the splits in front of her. He took off his cap and bowed his head. 'My God,' she laughed. 'What have we here.'

'You aint seen nothing yet lady. Let the show begin.' Before she had recovered, he zipped to his feet, handed her his cap and did three consecutive hand springs. He then completed his act with a standing somersault. Arms spread wide, he bowed low and holding his position, looked up at her with a 'how's that?' grin.

Open mouthed, she stood there amazed. Gleefully she clapped her hands. A couple of joggers nearby had virtually stopped in their tracks as they witnessed the demonstration... they joined in with appreciative hand clapping. Jargodin looked at them and acknowledged them with a smile and a wave of thanks.

Paula ran up to him, threw her arms around him, and gave him a kiss. 'My God, what have I got myself into? He's a bloody acrobat,' she laughed. 'Come on,' she murmured. 'You're coming back to the motel for a decent workout.' Their laughter could be heard all the way back to their room.

A strong affinity had developed between them. They had found each other...that was all that mattered...they were commited. Jargodin insisted he would return to Coober Pedy alone. He would return frequently using the small air service, (opal air), that operated between the two towns. Paula wanted to return with him...there was something he hadn't told her....this she knew.

'Look. there is nothing to keep me here in Adelaide. Why can't I come back with you. I can keep my flat. I have the money to pay for it...money is not a problem.'

'Darling. Let me go back and sort a few things out and get organised. Then you come up...it wont be long.'

'Jargodin,' her mouth tightened. 'Now is the time to tell me. Is there another woman? If there is, say so now. It will break my heart, but I would sooner be the victim now than being made a fool of altogether. Tell me truthfully Jargodin,' she whispered.

He tilted her chin, then put his arms on her waist. Their eyes locked. 'I swear on my mother's life, there is no other woman and I swear, there will be no other woman. You are my woman and I would die for you.' He gently kissed her lips.

She knew he was telling the truth. She knew that for a person from that European background, an oath on their mother's life was the ultimate. She also knew he was telling the truth...She just knew.

Right, she thought. You just don't know us Sicilian women. I'm not finished yet. Maybe I'll just load up the car and arrive up there unannounced. You are mine you bloody villiano...Let's wait and see.

The morning of departure had arrived. They were packed and ready. Jargodin had one more thing to do. He had to ring Johnny and let him know where he was staying for his guns to be delivered. There was a small parking bay in Glen Osmond road, between Greenhill road and South Terrace...that would do fine, eliminating any connection with the motel and his name.

'Paula, I have to make a phone call. I have to pick up a parcel on the way. It's now nine o'clock. What say we leave here at nine thirty, that will give us time for a cup of coffee, I'll ring a cab later to pick you up and you can leave from here. Okay?'

She numbly nodded her head. She was already feeling the loss. She listened as Jargodin picked up the phone and asked the receptionist to get him the number he quoted...' That was Johnnies number...She knew it by heart.'

Jargodin did not want her to know about the guns and Johnnies involvement. He didn't realise that Paula would recognise the number when he gave it to reception.

'This is Jargodin here , yes, fine. Look would it be possible to have those

things to be dropped off at that small parking bay in Glen Osmond road just past Greenhill road on the way to the city. That is on my way and I have to be out of the room here shortly. Say anytime from nine forty-five onwards. Yeah, thanks,' he laughed, 'yes I......'
The phone was taken out of his hands.

'Johnny?'

'Holy Jesus! Paula! Is that you? Oh, Jesus Christ! We've been out of our minds wondering where you were. June has been ringing your place for two days. You didn't come yesterday....Oh, God, no...don't tell me! Please Paula, say it is not true...Jeez...you're with Jargodin. I'll cut that bastard's throat. Paula...What's the name of the motel?'

Paula was taken back. She looked at Jargodin.

'What's wrong. Johnny is furious...He...he wants to know the name of the motel...What's the matter Jargodin?' She was bewildered at Johnnies tirade. Jargodin's eyes narrowed.

He nodded. 'Tell him.'

She was barely audible as she told Johnny the name. I'll be there in fifteen minutes...'

Jargodin could hear every word. He grabbed the phone..'Come easy Johnny..' He put the phone down.

Paula had turned pale. 'What was that all about?'

Jargodin gave her a steady look. 'He doesn't approve of me as fit company for you.'

'Has he reason to?'

'In a way, yes. I guess he has.' He put his hand up. 'Don't worry. I'm not wanted by the police or anything like that. I haven't got a criminal record, but let's just say, he doesn't approve of me being suitable company for you."

Paula sat on the bed. 'Oh, shit,' she said. 'I knew there was more to you than you told me. I can pick them! Well, let's see what happens. I think I'll need another coffee, in fact, I think I'm going to need more than a cup of coffee.'

Jargodin opened the door and left it ajar. They both sat on the far bed quietly sipping their coffee. 'Hey, don't worry, sweetheart. Everything is okay." He put his arm around her and gave her a squeeze. 'You should be grateful for the fact you have such wonderful friends.' No wonder he's mad, he thought. Jesus!

They had not long to wait. By now, Jargodin was sitting on the twin bed farthermost from the door. Paula was opposite him on the other bed. The side table between them held their cigarettes, coffee cups and ash tray. Paula leant towards him. She spoke quietly and firmly. 'Okay, lover boy. You're holding out on me. Why is Johnny in such a flap?'

Just then Jargodin looked up. Her head turned following his gaze...Johnny stood in the doorway.

'Ciao. Come in and close the door,' Jargodin said.

Johnny did as bidden, then stood there looking at them. The message was loud and clear. He put his hand to his head. 'Madre Mio. Paula,' he said, his brow furrowed in consternation. 'We have been out of our mind. June has been ringing and ringing. We didn't know what the hell to think. You understand what I mean. We thought they had come down from the north and we were at our wit's end.'

'Oh, God, Johnny,' Paula suddenly realised they had thought her parents had come down and whisked her away. 'Oh, hell, Johnny. I am sorry.'

'Yes, but now I find it is bloody worse. Here you are with this guy.' He nodded at Jargodin and spoke to him. 'You're all set to go back to Coober Pedy?' Jargodin nodded. 'Good. That's good, then this little affair can be forgotten.'

'Hold it Johnny. I'm a big girl now. Haven't I got any say in this matter?'

'Paula, you don't know this guy. He's up to no good. For God's sake forget him...Okay, you're both healthy young animals and I can understand the physical attraction. By the look of it you've had a ball. Let it be. No more. He goes back to doing God knows what and you forget him. You get on with your life. You deserve someone better than this 'villiaco.' Jargodin eyes half closed at the uttering of the word.

'Sorry Johnny. This is the begining, not the end.'

He turned to Jargodin. 'Look if you have any decency at all and I somehow think you have, go away and let this girl be. You have had your fun. Put another notch in your belt and go back north. Finito.'

'You'll have to do better than that Johnny. I love him and that is all there is to it. He's .....'

'Love...what the bloody hell, love!...Sure he's an attractive and intriguing guy. You have been lonely. As for him, all he wanted was a woman to sleep with..Okay.. Forget him...sometimes it's good for the soul...capise?'

'Look, for her sake tell her what you are.' Jargodin just looked at him not saying a word.

'Oh, Jesus, Paula, he's a bloody Al Capone!' Johnny exploded. The reaction he got was not what he expected. She stood, her mouth half opened and looked from one to the other.

'Truthfully?' she asked Johnny. He nodded dumbly. He had fired his last shot.

CHAPTER 13.

She threw back her head and laughed. 'Oh, how bloody priceless,' she exclaimed. 'How priceless.' She sat down on the bed opposite Jargodin. 'You,' she chuckled. 'A bloody Al Capone. Oh, Madonna! This is all too much...it is just too, too, divine....' She took control of herself. 'Fate,' she whispered .

Jargodin looked on in admiration and fascination as the transformation unfolded. She stood up defiantly, a hard gleam in her eyes.

'Al Capone,' she sneered. 'My family have been Al Capones for years...for generations. Half the God fathers came from my village. Do you think us Sicilian women are stupid?' she snarled. 'Where do you think all our bloody money came fron? A few grape vines on the side of a mountain over there. The countryside would be flat out supporting a few goats. Do you think the women don't know? Do you think they don't talk? Even as kids growing up we heard plenty we weren't supposed to hear and know.

'Why are the women always in church,

always praying? Why? Because they know and they hope their prayers will keep them safe from 'lupara.' 'Lupara,' avenge by a shot-gun blast. Go to Ingham in North Queensland, my home town and still see how many Italian farm houses are surrounded by high wire fences...go and see the Geese they have running free around their houses...Geese, the best watchdogs you can get.

Here was the female wildcat a product of generations of women who had worked, starved, cheated, lied, killed and were killed beside their husbands. They grew up in a land so barren that when Girabaldi and his troops conquered Sicily he looked around and said, 'how can anything live here. Give it back to them.' Here was the Sicilian female who would fight tooth and nail for her man. For the first time in her life the flood gates had been released.

'And, what about you Johnny. How much blood have you got on your hands. Don't get me wrong, I love you and June and your children, but let's face facts, your not quite lily white and June knows that..You're like my father. He dresses in the best, drives the latest car, is always smiling and nice to people...a pillar of the new society up north. He's up to his neck in prostitution in Brisbane and Sydney and God knows what else. You men, in your holier than though attitudes and your self-justification.

'Well, if I have an Al Capone for my man, then I am going to stand by him, as my mother did, as my grandmother did, and their mothers before them. Do you think I am stupid, 'a testa di azzino?' I knew there was something. Things have changed now. The plans are different. I am going with him. He will need me. He will need a cool head and I have that...I have animal cunning.' She looked at Jargodin. 'There will not be anything to do with drugs or prostitution....it will be opal.' She was right on target.

Paula sat down. She was drained of all emotion. Both men were taken back by her verbal onslaught. Johnny had noticed a bottle of whisky on the table when he first arrived. 'Jesu,' he said. 'I need a drink.'

Jargodin went to the refrigerator and took out two stubbies of beer. He opened them and gave one to Paula. Johnny had by this time poured himself a large scotch and was sipping it neat. Paula gave Jargodin a lop-sided grin as he handed her the stubbie. He smiled back in encouragement.

'Another thing,' Paula continued in a quieter tone. 'Look what is ahead of me if I stay here. It will not be long before my father or someone else arrives with an ultimation, that I must rejoin the fold. How long can I hold out...I have been through enough as it is. I don't want to be an outcast from my family, but that is what it boils down to...I either go back and marry some creep they have selected for me, or, keep running. There is a limit as to my strength on my own. I would sooner be dead..

Johnny shook his head. He looked at Jargodin. You're a cool bastard he thought. You haven't said a word.

Jargodin spoke, he thought he'd best get one thing straightened out. 'That parcel we talked about. I swear on oath no-one...no-one will be killed with them. I am not a killer. I am not goin to say, if the occasion arises that no-one will be harmed, but, that will be only in extreme circumstances.' Paula, not knowing the gist of the conversation, looked from one to the other. Johnny just nodded slowly.

'Well, I hope you have enough bloody

brains to realise the result if you think you can go around playing cowboys and indians. Oh, Jesus, what a bloody mess. I think I'll retire and grow tomatoes. I've got to sit.' He took a chair, noticed his empty glass, refilled it and sat down. 'I don't normally drink in the mornings, but since running into you,' he looked at Jargodin, 'it's becoming a habit.'

Johnny looked at Paula. 'You're sure you know what you are doing?' She nodded. 'Okay, let's, have a look at things and see what we can do.' The Godfather had taken over....

'For the last time, why don't both of you take you chances and disappear, even go overseas.' No-one spoke. 'Okay,' he sighed. 'Don't say I didn't try.' I don't know what is going to happen or how long you'll last, but I pity the poor bastards you come up against, he thought.

'Now you are sure you want to go to Coober Pedy, Paula?' She nodded. 'Okay, both of you better stay another day or two until we fix up a few things.' He looked at Jargodin. 'Today you meet my solicitor and make out a will in Paula's favour.' Paula started to speak, but he held up his hands. 'No ifs. or buts.'

Jargodin nodded.

'Paula, you keep your flat. Get another key cut and give it to me, and, go out and see June and the kids and tell them you are going to Coober Pedy for a holiday. Let's not worry her too much. We then have the problem of your family. Does Jargodin know?' His eyes swept from one to the other. Paula nodded.

"Right, they are going to come after you; you know that. I will try and stall things if I can, but they will find out where you are and who you are with...count on it. When they do, holy bloody hell. We will have to be ready for that or ready for a quick exit. How long do you intend to stay in Coober Pedy? he asked Jargodin.

'I have been four months checking this out; perhaps another four, five or six months...maybe more. Who knows could be much less. We will have to play it by ear.'

'Have you started doing anything about it yet?'

'Yes, sure.'

'Successful?'

Jargodin grinned. 'You could say that, and no-one is any the wiser.'

No doubt about it, Johnny thought.

You're a cool bastard.'You know, it is possible to make big money, just by honest mining up there,' Johnny said.

'Sure, I know, and who is to say that , that is not what I am doing? The only thing now is, we will have to take into consideration the mafia. This could add a sense of urgency.'

'It could add a sense of urgency alright,' the older man said. 'You had better believe it. You know what they are likely to do to you?'

Jargodin nodded. 'Yeah, I know,' he chuckled.

'Oh, God, I never thought of that. Jargodin, I know them. They'll kill you. I can't have that.'

He took her hands and looked at her. 'Don't worry about me. I'll be okay. If you want to come with me, that is all that matters, Together we will beat the bastards.' Paula just nodded. Johnny, looking on, thought, you know, you cheeky so and so, I think you just might, but how, I don't know.

'If I want to get in touch with you, I'll leave a message at Ruffoes. Remember anytime you ring me, your phone call has to go through the Woomera exchange and that the Federal Police are in charge of Woomera. There is only one bank in the town so don't have too much in an account there.'

'Already taken care of, I have another account in a bank down here.'

'Now, about your parcel. I want two thousand now. When you are ready to leave it will be outside your door here. There will be no fingerprints on it and a bodgie name care of the 'Miner's store Coober Pedy. Someone you met at the club asked you to drop if off for them. Okay?'

'Hell,' Paula said. 'This seems like a scene from the untouchables.'

'It might well end up being a true untouchable series, believe me,' Johnny said seriously.

CHAPTER. 14.

The dug-out had been transformed from a miner's camp to a pleasant home. Jargodin had thrown his hands up in mock despair at Paula's complete cleaning and re-arranging. New pieces of furniture were purchased. She was proud of their dug-out and fascinated by the fact that they were actually living in a cave in the side of a hill.

To her, everything about the frontier town was fascinating; the wind generators, or free lights as they were called, never ceased to amaze her. The fact that each dug-out had its own source of power was to her, incredible. She had never seen such a melting pot of nationalities in such a small community. Aboriginals formed quite a proportion of the population and the sight of groups of them aimlessly sitting in the dust, all sharing bottles or flagons of alcohol, disturbed her greatly. To her mind, this was the only blot on the landscape. She loved the wide open style of life, the freedom, but most of all there was a feeling of excitement in the town.

The sixteen mile field just recently found was proving a bonanza beyond the wildest dreams of many. The seventeen mile field was flourishing as well as the other more well known ones. Coober Pedy was in boom mode. Everybody seemed to have money and plenty of it; if you were not one of the fortunate ones, your friends were never hesitant to help. Daily, tales were told of big parcels of opal being found.

The hotel and clubs were continually packed ; the gambling tables ran hot; card games of Manila attracted big money; the motel units were booked on a permanent basis by Chinese buyers with unlimited money to purchase Australian opal.

It was impossible not to be caught up in the air of excitement: Paula felt more alive than she had ever been in her life; to add to it all, she was so much in love with a rogue who was, as exciting as the town itself.

Paula felt she was part of the whole scene. Jargodin took her out to the fields, driving around the tracks that wound in and out around the mounds of sandstone dirt brought up from underground. She was soon conversant with the mining operations.

She, 'Noodled,' side by side with other men and women, black and white alike, for the misplaced pieces of opal that came up in buckets from the winches, or dropped from the hoppers of the blowers. The blowers, or, as a lot of people said, should be called suckers, were set up on the back of trucks. Large diesel motors drove a series of belts that created suction into a line of nine inch galvanised pipes. These pipes went underground to the 'face,' where men worked and blasted. The loose dirt was shovel fed into these pipes and sucked up into the hoppers above. When the hoppers had reached their load, a flap opened and the dirt dropped out.

When the dirt fell, the noodlers were waiting and would quickly stream through the loose ground with their fingers searching for pieces of the precious stone. The fields being rich, a lot of the miners were generous and, at times, careless. A lot of good opal reached the noodlers. It was possible to make good money.

Noodlers would wander from one claim to another until they came to one, 'on opal,' and there they would squat in the dirt an go to work. Miners on opal would tell their friends and soon word of mouth would let you know where to search.

Women were scarce in Coober Pedy and it was not long before an attractiive girl like Paula was well known by her presence. Dressed always in jeans, a loose long sleeved top and large brimmed straw beach hat, as she was rather proud of her milk white skin, she stood out from the tanned seasoned locals. Known as Jargodin's girl, it was hands off; the majority of guys were decent types, but lonely. It was good therefore to be her friend and receive a cheery wave and a pleasant word from her; it felt good to be recognised by an attractive woman.

Paula had great childish delight with the opal she was finding. At night they would clean it and put it in bottles of water. She never ceased to marvel at the beauty and colours it reflected; she never tired of picking up the bottles, holding them up to the light to see them at their best. The days were good...the nights were better.

It was mid-morning and as usual hot. Summer was well under way. Very few of the miners would work beyond one or two o'clock. Paula and Jargodin were sitting side by side, happily sifting dirt through their fingers on one of the dumps. There were a scattering of people all doing the same thing; they were mainly women and all knew each other...if not, it didn't matter...you still spoke to each other.

'Hey Jargodin!'

He looked over into the mischevious eyes of a crone like Croation woman a few yards away. Equal to the occasion, for he knew it would be light-hearted banter, he took off his cap in respect, nodded, and asked, 'yes madame.'

Everybody, huge smiles on their faces, stopped and listened, anticipating the fun. The Croation woman, black scarf over her head and knotted under the chin and wearing a typical peasant shapeless dress, gave a toothless gum chuckle.

'My husband, Duschin, you know Duschin?'

'Ah, yes, of course I know Duschin...Ah...now I know why he is so happy always. I see now what a lucky man he is...You are his wife...Mama Mio.' Everybody laughed, including the old crone.

'Well, he say to me, 'we don't see Jargodin down the club now. Before he

always there. Now, no more. I say to him, maybe he got better things to do.'
There was laughter all around.

'Duschin say to me, 'you know he was good company and told us funny stories and sometimes he do jumps. You know...' She waved her hands in confusion as she sought in vain for the right English words...'Basta,' she muttered...'the...you know...jump, jump... like, you jump... inside out!' Gales of laughter swept the group.

The showman came to the fore. He gave Paula a quick wink. With a grim look on his face, he stood up, reached down and helped Paula rise and guided her down the side of the small dump on to solid ground. The laughter had stopped...There was silence and embarrassment...What had gone wrong? The poor Croation woman was upset.

'Let's away from here,' Jargodin sternly said. They walked in silence for about ten metres, then without pause he threw himself backwards, completing three backward somersaults. Turning to the spectators, he did the splits, and taking off his cap, which he had previously set firmly on his head, he bowed to the startled old lady. 'Madame, for you, I jump, inside out, anytime.'

They laughed and clapped, thrilled with the scene that had taken place out here in the outback. Duschin's wife had a day she would never forget...a day to remember. Jargodin became known as the guy who, would jump... inside out.

Word spread quickly. Often people sang out to him: 'Hey, Jargodin, jump inside out for us.' Invariably he would perform something and if the request was from children, he found it almost impossible to resist. He was forever the showman.

Paula, proud of his prowess, was still laughing as he zipped to his feet. 'More, more,' they cried as Paula took his arm

'No, no more,' she said, 'I am taking him home where he can jump inside out for me.' This sent them into further gales of laughter.

'It seems a shame to rob some of these people.' The evening meal over, they were sitting quietly sipping a cup of coffee.

Jargodin looked at Paula. 'For a start, Paula, we are not going to rob, as you put it, just anyone. Don't be fooled. A lot of those bastards, would cut your throat quick smart if they thought, it was to their benefit. There are some very nasty characters out there and these are the ones we will target. Don't forget, we have 'The Family,' haunting us in the background. I'm afraid there is no room for sentiment here. You have to trust me. There are a few Muslims and a few Greeks I have some settling with: I'm sorry sweetheart...You know it is not too late for you to go back.' He held her gaze.

She leant across the table and touched his hand. 'I'm with you all the way...All I ask is, we try not to hurt anyone, nor rob anyone who badly needs money, and, we get what we can, in as quick a time as we can, so we can disappear somewhere and make a good life.' He nodded.

'Agreed. Fron now on we have to start watching carefully. We have to take note of who we think is on opal and take particular notice of the location of the shafts on the claims.

'The sixteen mile field, usually has big runs and if they are getting opal, they could be on it, sometimes, for weeks. In a lot of the other fields, the pockets can be small and can be taken out in a day, or two days.

'We know. that where the noodlers are sitting on dumps picking up chips and pieces, that they must be getting opal down below. That is a dead give-away. Take notice when they are knocking off work, how and when they are pulling up gear from underground: if they are bringing up opal, you will notice how they pull one bag up with extreme care. Invariably then they will hasten to their vehicle, put it in and quickly cover it with some bags or rags. Also take note of those who leave their claims early. They've got a strike and are high-tailing it to town to clean and sell.

'Don't worry, darling, it will be as I said before, mainly the Muslims, Greeks and Serbians, who will pay the price: some of them have a lot to answer for,' As he spoke these words, Jargodin realised that he was now trying to justify himself with the ethnic hatred that had been handed down through the centuries. The sins of our fathers, he thought.

With mixed emotions, Paula nodded. She accepted her lot.

CHAPTER 15.

Paula insisted. "I have come into this with my eyes open. I am part of it; besides, I would be worried sick just waiting. I can stay up top and watch."

Jargodin knew he would have no choice. He accepted the fact. They worked out a system of warning.

A strong thin line would be let down the shaft and a billy-can tied to the end. Five or six reasonable size stones would then be put in the can. If there was any reason for alarm, Paula would jerk the rope up and down quickly a few times. They tried it out. It worked.

Dressed in dark clothing, they would leave the dug-out at varied times after midnight.

"My, God, I have never been so frightened," she laughed. They had just returned from their first nightly escapade. She was still in a state of exhiliration. The adrenalin was still pumping. "I was sure every shadow moved and I was hearing noises that weren't there. You seemed to be down below for hours, when, in reality, you were only there for twenty minutes."

Jargodin looked at her. "Paula, you don't have to come anymore. I would be happier if you stayed at home."

"No way, Hosay! Sure, I was scared, but I was excited; I found a side of me I never knew existed. We are in this together lover boy!" Jargodin shrugged helplessly.

Four more raids over the next two weeks had resulted in a sizeable amount of opal. Paula found, that with each trip, the apprehension she felt, heightened her awareness. she turned this to advantage. They continued to go out to the fields during the day, seeing and being seen. As everyone else on the fields, they heard the talk of the night time thefts. The amounts stolen were told to be of astronomical proportions. It was decided to lay low for a while.

Jargodin had bought a tumbler and a set of sieves for the cleaning process. He had tumbled all the opal in water for a half hour, then scraped, snipped, and cleaned the dirt, potch and sandstone from the precious gem. He had finished putting it all through his set of seives, seperating the sizes when Josef arrived to do the classing.

Josef, dressed as usual in singlet, shorts and thongs, came through the dug-out door with a ready smile. His eyes lighted on the opal spread on the table before hiom.

"Phew," he whistled. "Someone has been lucky....or....busy." He looked at Paula then Jargodin, who was in the process of handing him the ritual stubbie in greeting. Paula looked at Jargodin. They both were now certain....Josef knew. Jargodin pointed to a chair. They both sat.

"Good luck." Josef raised his stubbie and took a sip. He leant forward and spoke quietly as his grey eyes went from one to the other. "I class both of you as family, so what I am saying is for your benefit. I am led to believe that you, Jargodin, my friend, are the mysterious moonlighter." He laughed. "If so, I say good luck to you...I only wish I was with you. Let me add to that. This is the amazing part...Both of you are the mysterious moonlighters."

Paula paled as she listened. Jargodin showed no outward signs, but his brain was racing...how the hell, does he know, or is he guessing?

"I must stress, your secret is safe with me; but then, how do I know, or am I just guessing?" He grinned. "Sit back folks and listen how Sherlock Holmes of the outback came to this conclusion..

"Some of the miners who were done over became irate, went to the police and kicked up a stink. The police had to do something. You know that elderly aboriginal who is always sitting in the lane next to the miner's store. A group of them sit there cleaning bits of opal they have noodled. He is a tall thin guy with a bit of a grey beard. A quiet guy. His wife is that fat one called Rosy. You can hear her a mile away. She is always talking or laughing. You know the ones I mean. I have seen you stop and chat with them many a time. I have seen you give them money...Maybe now your kind deeds are being rewarded."

"That tall thin fellow is probably the best black-tracker in the country. Some of the things he has done have been amazing. Do you know about these guys?"

"I have heard about them, yes."

Paula nodded. "Yes, we have them up in North Queensland."

"The police in their wisdom, decided to take old Charlie out and let him look around these claims that have been robbed. They took him out to the four of them. 'Too many people been walking here boss,' he told the police."

"Charlie sent word yesterday he wanted to see me. I thought he must have wanted money. I caught up with him just before I came here. He knows we are close friends.

"Yes I know the ones you mean." He turned to Paula. "Remember when you first arrived and we were walking past that group of Aboriginees and we stopped. I introduced you to Rosy. Remember, I said to her,'Hey Rosy, you my number two girl now. This one my number one. Remember? Rosy nearly went into hysterics."

Paula laughed. "Yes, I remember."

"Well, these aboriginees know a person's footprint just as we know a face. Charlie took me aside and told me about the police and his trip out to the field. 'Jargodin, that one good friend of yours and good friend of Rosy and me, he bin there. I see footprints all the same him and smaller one all same Mrs. Jargodin.

"You sure Charlie, I asked him. 'No gammon Josef,'" he said. "Maybe you tell Jargodin eh? I bin see him fella footmark, then I bin walk big circle way out. I see where he walk to mine. Each one. I see tracks. I tell policeman, no good. Too many fella walk there. When I come back, I get one cousin, Tommy. Him fella got car. He bin drive me to Seventeen mile field where police take me. I have good look around. I follow track all way back to where they leave car. I do same sixteen mile field. No trouble for Charlie."

"So, there it is. Word for word as Charlie told me. It pays to be kind to people." Josef sat back. "Tell me to mind my own business, or that I am crazy, but I had to tell you."

They were silent. Jargodin looked at Paula then back to Josef. He nodded. "Yes, it was us. Who would have thought of the black-trackers."

Josef nodded in agreement. They can track you over solid rock, those guys."

"We were going to ask you if you would like to be in it with us. We weren't sure."

Josef paused before he spoke. "I would like to get out. I have made a lot of money, but, I have nothing to show for it. I am sick and tired of mining on the off chance. I think," he said with a smile, "I would rather let someone else find it and then go down for my share." They laughed.

"Right, you are in, amigo." They shook hands.

"What about Charlie?" Paula asked.

"Do not worry," Josef said. "I gave him $50. He wont say a word."

"Thanks." Jargodin pulled a roll of

$50 notes from his pocket and gave one to Josef. "We will have to be more careful."

Paula shook her head. "Madonna! Too close for comfort."

"They would never be able to prove anything. The trouble is everybody would know and you would cop all sorts of flak. Never mind, by the look of the table here, you have a nice little haul. Let me get stuck into it; there is a lot of sorting to be done.

It was late afternoon before the opal was sorted, weighed and classed. Josef stood up, arched his back and stretched his arms wide. He threw cold water on his face. Classing needed concentration.

"Let's sell and get it over with. Jackson Lou is here. He is a Chinese buyer, but pays a fair price." Jargodin nodded his agreement.

"Chicken and spaghetti when you return. How does that sound?" Paula asked.

Josef grinned. "There wont be any complaints from me."

Jargodin tipped the airline bag upside down on the kitchen table. Bundles of $50 bills fell out. Paula gasped. "Oooh...", she said. "How much?"

"80,000," Jargodin answered. He gave

Josef $8,000. "Thanks mate. You earned every cent of it." Josef nodded his thanks.

Jargodin picked up the remaining money, put it in the bag and hnded the bag to Paula. "Look after it sweetheart, will you?"

Paula took the bag and stared at him with a look of amazement. "Look after it, he says. The most money I have seen in my life and he says, 'look after it.' What am I going to do with it? I wont be able to sleep tonight. Where will I hide it? Under the bed?" They all laughed.

Josef sat back. "Paula, your cooking leaves me lost for words. How am I ever going to eat at Ruffoes again?" Like all good cooks, praise was the ultimate reward. Josef would always be welcome.

They sat drinking coffee. "We lay low for a while. What we want is to find someone on a big run of opal. It is better to get one big haul. The risks are less than a lot of small results. I have been thinking," Jargodin continued. "We should buy some gym shoes or desert boots about two sizes bigger than we normally wear. We put on two pair of thick woollen socks to take up the slack. After each job we throw them down these test holes around the place. It's a small price to pay.

They sat silent thinking it over..."Good idea," Josef said. Paula nodded in agreement. It had been a big day. Paula was soon asleep, her last thoughts of the $70,000 in the oven of the gas oven.

"Why are you stopping here?"

Jargodin pointed to a car outside a dug-out. For sale, $1,000 was printed on the back window. "Hang on a moment Paula. I wont be long." She watched as Jargodin knocked on the door of the dug-out. A man came out. Jargodin pointed to the car.

He smiled at her as he leant on the door. "I just bought it. Do me a favour honey? You drive our car and park in front of the restaurant. I will follow in this one." He stood back. "I will park in front of the Shell service station. Wait for me in the car."

"Why did..."

"I will explain when we get there." He leant forward, gave her a quick kiss and laughed as he ran over to the battered early model Holden he had just purchased.

Paula and Jargodin walked back to the lane beside the Miner's store. They heard Rosies shrill voice before they got there. There were about fifteen aboriginees in the group. They sat around, children, Aunts and Uncles comprising the family kin. Charlie was there. He looked up at Jargodin. He gave his usual smile.

"Palya?" Jargodin asked.

"Uwa," Charlie nodded.

"What about you Rosie, my number two girl. Palya?"

"Aieee," Rosie shrieked. "Jargodin, you make gammon. Aieee." They all laughed.

"Hey, Jargodin," a young black face with a broad grin and dazzling white teeth asked, "You jump inside out for us?" This brought more laughter.

"Not today, Bunjy. I got to talk some business with my number one girl.

"Aieee," they rocked back and forth. Jargodin and Paula managed to extract Rosie and Charlie and lead them up the road to the Holden he had just bought. He gave Charlie the key.

"Yours Charlie."

The tall gaunt aboriginee's opened wide. "For true?"

"For true, Charlie. For you and Rosie. Here are the papers. You go to the Police station and fix him up. He's all yours Charlie. If you have any problems, you take him to the garage. They fix him and I pay."

"Eeee is for true. This car for Rosie and Charlie?" Rosie asked. Jargodin nodded.

Rosie looked at Paula. "You no tell me lie," then a big grin spread over her round face. "Hey, number one, you no gammon, eh?"

Paula bent close to Rosie and said quietly, "no gammon number two." The other aboriginees had followed Charlie and Rosie aware something was happening. They were now gathered around grinning and laughing.

Rosie tried to take charge. "Eh, Charlie, you too old to drive. Better me drive."

Charlie refused to be upstaged on this momentous occasion. "You no drive! You never bin drive. I drive." Charlie quickly got into the driver's seat. Rosie hurried around to the passenger seat.

Jargodin lent through the window and pointed out the position of the gears. "You will be okay Charlie. After a few times, no problem. Charlie, now full of concentration, nodded.

Paula and Jargodin stood well back.

The motor gave a roar, the car leapt forward and stopped. It leapt forward again and stopped. The motor cut out each time. Rosies shrill screams could be heard above the motor which had been started once again.

A few more jerky hops and the car sped off down the highway. The bystanders, including, Paula and Jargodin, laughed and clapped. Paula gripped Jargodin's arm. "Oh, God," she said, "That was priceless. I love you, you bastard, I never know what you are going to do next. Amid the slaps on the back from the amazed and happy bystanders, arm and arm they left the scene.

"Talking about next, my darling, we go to Opal Air. We're booking two flights to Adelaide. We have business down there.

---------------CHAPTER 16. ----------------

Paula laughed as she looked around her Adelaide flat. "Yes," she said. "It's nice, but, I love our dug-out; it's so different and unique. It is like Coober Pedy...There is no other place like it in the world.

Johnny smiled across at Paula. "I must say, it certainly agrees with you. I have not seen you looking so radiant. June was excited when your call came through; so were the kids, Juanata and Ric. They insist you come out tomorrow afternoon and stay for dinner. Okay? He looked from Paula to Jargodin. They both nodded.

"I had to come to the city on business, but I thought I had best see you first. Any problems up there?"

"No...none Johnny," Jargodin said. "We managed to pick up a bit of money and we have some shopping to do. It seemed a good idea to get away for a week or so." Johnny nodded knowing there was a lot more to be told. It would come later.

"Johnny, I need about four walkie-talkies. The best on the market. Any ideas?"

"No problem. A friend of mine is well up in electronics. Leave it with me. You said you picked up some money. How much? I do not want to be nosy, but you may have to spend a few dollars...nothing much."

"No worries paisano...We picked up a little over $70,000." Johnnies eyebrows lifted.

"M'mm. Not bad. Paula would you mind if if I had another coffee please. I want you both to listen carefully to what I have to say. It is important."

"Certainly Johnny. I'll get us all one. Una momento."

They sat sipping their cups of coffee waiting for Johnny to continue. "You must keep in mind Paula's family. You can be sure they know what is happening; if they don't, it wont be long before they do. We have to be prepared for any sort of action, at a moment's notice."

"I want both of you to go out to the cemetry...don't look surprised. You walk around until you find a tombstone of a young child who was born within a year or two of yourselves. The important thing is that the name is of ethnic origin. . Let us keep it as close to reality as possible.

"When you have found what you want, write down the particulars of the tombstone. Next go to 'The Advertiser,' in the city. You will then have to search through the funeral notices corresponding with what you have. This could be a long and tedious process, as the tombstone may only have the year of the death. You might have to go through a full year of papers...hat is hardly likely.

"check the funeral notices and get all the particulars. Everything. With this information we write and ask for a birth certificate. We sign a family name and I have an address we can use. When we have these birth certificates, I will do the rest. I will driver's licences and passports. I will fix it so that you are clean with the tax department. All this will cost a bit of money, but it is important to be prepared. This way, we have new identities and passports at our fingertips...if need be."

"I'll be stuffed!" Jargodin exclaimed. "So that is how it's done."

Paula chuckled. "Johnny, Zio, you are one crafty man. Where did you learn these things?"

Johnny smiled. "So, now I am Zio, eh?

Uncle. To answer your question, I went to night school."

"I'll bet! I guess it was not the kind of night school I went to," Paula added.

"No, I am afraid not. It was the university of hard knocks. It was amazing what you have to learn to survive," he said.

"Well, you must have learnt your lessons well. Look at you. You look a million dollars; immaculate tailor made suits, alligator shoes, a rolex watch that must be worth a fortune. No wonder June fell for you."

"Ha! When I met June, I had nothing. I arrived here in Adelaide with five pounds in my pocket. I was lucky" He turned to Jargodin. "Like you, I could speak English. That was my greatest asset. I started work on a large building site as a labourer. .there was a number of New Australians employed there. I soon became the interpreter and go between for them. It was there I met June. She worked in the office. I could not believe this gorgeous Australian girl would have anything to do with me."

"I was blessed. She became my teacher and guide. I owe her everything. We got married. We saved our money and invested in land. I bought and sold a couple of small businesses. Los of new arrivals came to me for help and advice.

"we bought a new home and things were rather good, We now had two young children. Property values were going up and i was doing well. I could see the sprawl of development coming and bought a lot of land far out, at give away prices. I say, 'ar out,' but now they are rated as close to town. I made a lot of money."

"Then the past reared its ugly head. I started to get visits from some of the leaders of the Ustashia" He looked from Paula to Jargodin, his eyes half closed in recollection. The bastards wanted me to donate money for their cause...for Croatia, and all the rest of the bullshit they justified themselves with. I told them that this was my country now. I had married an Australian girl, was naturalised and classified myself as an Australian. I wanted no part of any bloody trouble overseas. That was why I left.

"Nothing happened for a couple of months. There was a coffee lounge in town that I would always drop into; it was owned by a friend of mine. This day they had me set up. I had no sooner walked in and sat down when these two characters came in, straight to my table. They sat down opposite me. I knew them both...bad bastards....hit men. I was lucky. It was ten o'clock in the morning and the cafe was empty. Tony, the owner, had seen me come in and was all set to come around and say, hello, when he saw these other guys. He stopped and watched. He knew something was wrong the way it happened. He pretended to be busy, but, watching us all the time. I could depend on Tony. We were close friends."

"To cut a long story short, these goons told me that a donation of $5,000 was thought to be a fitting sum for the fight back in Jugoslavia. It was also hinted that my family could end up with health problems if I did not come to the party. I was boiling inside. I had to do something drastic. These people only knew one language. If I weakened then, I would always be in their clutches.

"I pretended to be rattled and scared. Truth was, I was bloody scared. I told them I had no money on me but Tony was a friend of mine and maybe he could give me a couple of thousand now until I could arrange the balance. Well, if you could have seen the smug look on the faces of these peanuts. I walked over to Tony and whispered across the counter, 'the persuader Tony, give me the persuader.' Tony had a piece of rubber hose about thirty centimetres long filled with sand. He kept it under the counter. Any real trouble in the joint and Tony would come out swinging this bloody thing. He told me about a couple of times when he first opened up, how he had to use it. He called it his 'persuader.'"

"No more trouble since, Johnny, he would say. My persuader, he do the job. So here am I hoping to God, he gets the message. He does. He goes along the counter and rummages around. I look up in the wall mirror and I can see these guys grinning and whispering to each other. I can almost hear them say how easy it was. What a pushover I was.

"Tony slid the hose across to me. I was wearing a suit. I pushed it down inside my coat and holding it, walked back. These poor bastards thought I had money. They did not have a chance. I made a mess of them. The threat to my family sent me a little crazy I guess.

"The stupid bludgers each had a gun. They were out cold, both of them. I rang the police and spoke to a detective I knew. I also asked him to get in touch with the Federal cops as well. Tony closed the shop until they arrived. It all happened quickly. The police, ambulance and two Federal police arrived. No problem. They had been watching these two, as well as others for some time. It was a breakthrough for them. Tony swore black and blue he had seen them pull a gun on me.

"I knew what had happened was not enough. I had to go right to the top. I knew who the head man in the state was; a pillar of society...a building contractor with a huge business. He had come out here before me and had really made a name for himself. He was always in the news, donating to this fund, that fund, and of course, the church. He had a suite of offices here in the city.

"I bowled up to his offices, past his secretary and other staff straight into his room. He looked up at me and was speechless. I told him that I had already taken out two, not one, contracts on his life. If anything was to happen to me or any of my family, no matter how trivial, accident or other wise...he was dead.

"These men I have been in touch with, I stressed, have already received a token payment and they were professionals. They were not bungling amateurs like the ones he had sent on me. I have not had any problems since. His two thugs were deported after they came out of hospital. They must have talked as the Federal boys haunted the top guy for some time.

"So," Johnny sighed, "You have struck a nerve in my past. Apart from the fact, Paula has become family to us, I will do all in my power to help. Look at the grey hair coming through," he said as he fingered his hairline. "This...This is the result of trying to help shady characters like you two," he laughed. "No worries. I guess you remind me a lot of June and myself."

They sat silent. Jargodin went into the bathroom nd returned with two bundles of cash. "There is $10,000 there Johnny. Use what you have to and hang on to the rest. Who knows what expenses we may incur." Johnny nodded and put the money in his pockets.

Paula and I will go to the cemetry tomorrow morning and get the necessary particulars."

"Do that. It could take me a couple of months to get all the paper work done down here. I suggest when you return be as careful as you can. When I have your Visas, I think it would be a good idea to leave the country for a couple of years. I will do some checking as to possible destinations. We can discuss this later. I just hope," he looked at Paula, "your family hangs off a little longer. She nodded..

CHAPTER 17.

June and Paula were sitting in the kitchen drinking tea. The glass window gave an uninhibited view of the large backyard. The lawns, the barbecue, the swimming pool fitted comfortably in the spacious area.

June, what is your secret? You don't look a day older from when I first met you. You are still slim and trim. "Looks are deceiving, my dear. Oh, heavens, it looks as if my two adolescents have taken control of Jagodin." June was watching her daughter and son lead Jargodin around on a tour of the grounds. "Is that his first name Paula, or what?"

Paula laughed. "No, his name is Method Jargodin, but," she shook her head, "he insists he be called Jargodin...Just Jargodin."

"How strange, but then again, he is a strange man." June blushed. "Don't get me wrong. I did not mean that in a derogative sense. What I mean is...he is different. You look into those dark eyes and you wonder whether he is smiling with you or at you. He confuses you. His eyes are like a barrier. while he is summing you up, you can't get through;

then all of a sudden, it is as if a decision has been made... The barrier drops, the smile on his face then incleudes his eyes, and bang; you are let in. You are friends. Tell me, " June continued, "how is it really going up there on the opal fields?"

"It's great. I really love the place. You know, being up there with Jargodin, and the type of man he is, I can understand my mother better. I am learning to understand the Sicilian women." She held her friend'seyes. "I find myself in church a lot. Not praying for anything in particular, but just in church, either sitting or kneeling. There is this wonderful underground church. I seem to realise why the women of our family are as they are." She shrugged. "I guess it is the life style of our men," she whispered.

"There is one snag at the church. An Italian guy who lives net door to the church is a problem. I do not know what his role is. Apparently he keeps the church clean and looks after the general maintenance. He could be a lay brother for all I know. Every time I go there lately, he seems to appear. He hangs around pretending to be busy. He is a fat little greasy bastard, He has tried to talk to me a few times. I have ignored him. Most of the time he seems to be half drunk. You can smell the stale wine on his breath. The other day I was coming leaving when he stepped out of a small room near the entrance. I had to pass him. 'Paula,' he said. He spoke to me in Italian. I don't know how he got my name. 'Cara mio, how nice to see you.' He put his hand out to take one of mine. I saw red. Don't touch me you bastard, I said. I slipped past him out to the car."

"He sounds like a nice creep. Why don't you tell Jargodin?"

"Oh, God, no. Jargodin would kill him. No, I will handle it. It will blow over. He has the message."

"Would you like a drink love? Paula and I are having a cup of tea." June spoke as Johnny entered the kitchen.

"Yes, please. A cup of tea would be nice for a change. I drink too much coffee." He pulled out a chair and sat down. "Where is Jargodin?"

"Ric and Junata have captured him. OH, God," Paula said pointing through the windows. There was a horizontal bar in the yard and as they watched, Ric, a fit seventeen year, leapt up, grabbed the bar and started to swing.

June spoke quickly, thinking Paula was concerned for his safety. "He's okay. He goes to the gym three times a week. He often plays around on that bar."

Ric swung back and forth, his swings gradually increasing in depth. He let the bar go and did an open somersault, landing gracefully on the sandpit. Jargodin nodded his head in a, 'well done,' gesture. He thought awhile then mved under the bar. His hands by his sides he shook them in a loosening up exercise. "Oh, Madonna," said Paula with a smile.

"He wants to be careful," June said, full of concern.

Paula chuckled. "He'll be okay."

Jargodin leapt up, took hold of the bar, and arms fully extended, swung to and fro. His swings gathered momentum. At the top of a forward swing, he let go. With surprising speed he did a double tuck somersault and landed faultlessly. He then did two forward rolls...stood for a second...completed a back somersault...paused...turned to his young audience...did the splits and bowed his head.

Amazement would hardly be the word for the reaction. Ric and Junata stood spellbound at this unexpected display. Overcoming their shock they both clapped and laughed.

"The bastard has escaped from a cirus!" Johnny exclaimed. June was lost for words. A feeble, 'oh, my God,' was all she could say. Paula laughed. It was just another of Jargodin's surprises.

Jargodin spent the next twenty minutes as an instructor to Ric and Junata. He had won their hearts. It was late at night when Paulaand Jargodin left. The visit had been a success. They were family.

"Gawd," Ric said, after Paula and Jargodin had left. "He sure is full of surprises that Jargodin. I asked him where did he learn his gymnastics. It seemed like a cloud came over his face. He just shrugged and didn't answer. Do you know dad?" They all looked expectantly at Johnny.

Johnny thought a while. "What I tell you, goes no further." He looked at Ric and Junata. They nodded. "As a lad he was in a circus. His brother was a star...A trapeze artist. One day with no net, the catcher missed his brother. He was killed. Jargodin shot the catcher. You do not need to know anymore. Okay?"

"Oh, God," Junata said. "What a

terrible experience."

"Don't forget you two, you are bound to silence."

"Don't worry, dad. I love Paula like a sister and I like him also. I think he's great. It must have been awful for him. My lips are sealed."

"Same here dad. You know you can trust us."

"I know. I love you both, now off to bed. It has been a big day."

"Do you think they will make it Johnny?" June asked when they were alone.

"I don't know sweetheart. It's a tough one. It reminds me a lot of us when we were starting off." June nodded. "There is a big difference, however. This is Mafia...but," his face lit up in a boyish grin, "I think that bloody pair will come out smelling like roses."

June laughed. "I hope you're right, and knowing you, you will be doing all you can to help."

"We will wont we?" They both laughed.

CHAPTER. 018.

'Johnny rang last night. He wants me to come down to Adelaide for a couple of days. I am flying down this afternoon. I will be away two or three days. Did you tell him anything about us?'

Jargodin looked at his friend. He and Paula had arrived back in the mining town the day before. 'We talked about you. I told him you had done my classing and we were close friends. I did not think it was my place to say more than that.' Jargodin grinned. 'He told me, if I got into strife, you could be depended upon and you were the ideal guy to watch my back.'

Josef laughed. 'Yes, well, I think he is more concerned than he lets on. You are lucky to have him in your corner.'

Jargodin nodded seriously. 'We are extremely lucky. Don't worry, Paula and I realise that. We are more than grateful....'

'I will fly down today. I should be back by the end of the week. I have been out around the Sixteen mile field these last few days. Jeez, there is some opal coming out of that field. One claim is worthwhile watching, it is owned by a few Greeks.

'They have a claim almost in the centre of the field. I've been watching them for the past couple of days. I think they are on a big run, so much so, they have towed an old caravan on to the site. I don't know whether they intend to have someone sleeping there at night, or just to use it for storage. It's interesting. They must have confidence in the claim for them to do that. It might pay to keep our eyes on it.'

'I'll check it out while you're away.'

'It is easy to find. There are only a few caravans out there. Theirs is the only one in the centre of the field.'

'No worries paisano. You have a good trip. Give our regards to Johnny and the family. I have left Paula down at Luke's supermarket. I told her I would not be long. She sends her best and says, she will have a chicken and spaghetti dinner for you whenever you wish.'

'Great. Tell her to hold it until I get back.' The two friends shook hands.

Paula wanted time to re-arrange the dug-out. This suited Jargodin. He decided to check out the claim Josef referred to. At seven o'clock next morning he joined the string of cars heading out to the fields. A few months before the Sixteen mile field was a bare expanse. Len Butts sank a few Calwell drill holes for a miner who said, "why not here." It was proving to be one of the richest fields in history.

The field was about two kilometres off the main Seventeen mile road. The main area being worked was not much larger than one kilometre square. Every metre of ground within the area was pegged. It was a maze of mulloch heaps and machinery. Vehicles made their own tracks to their section of dirt. Later that day on their way out, a newly dug shaft with the accompanying pile of dirt would bar their way. A spin of the wheel, a slight detour, and, a new track was made.

Shafts were sunk...the Calwell machines were in demand. Their large corkscrew like drills would put a one metre wide circular hole down twenty metres in about three hours. All were impatient to get to the riches, hidden for millions of years.

Jargodin stopped at the edge of the field. He got out of his car, taking his

small pick with him. He looked back
towards the town. A continual cloud of
dust hung over the main road, the result
of the continual string of cars, trucks,
and utilities speeding out to their
claims. On a still morning the dust hung
like a thick cloud. Visibility was
limited, the drivers prayed for a cross
breeze to clear the road. It was
exciting... Today more fortunes would be
made.

Some noodlers were already on dumps
that had no doubt rewarded them the day
before. Men were piling out of their
vehicles. Generators and blowers were
being started. It was like a giant
octopus with the tentacles starting to
come alive. Within the hour it would be
a hive of activity. Jargodin stopped and
talked to some of the noodlers, said,
"hello," to some of the miners as he
made his way to the centre of the field.

The claim he was seeking was easy to
find. A sad four metre caravan stood on
one corner of the claim. He scrambled
half way up the slope of a large dump on
a neighbouring pegged area. He scooped
away the loose dirt to make a
comfortable sitting position. Here he
had a commanding view of the workings,
at the same time being inconspicuous.

A blower stood idle beside a shaft that the twenty centimetre galvanised pipes disappeared into. A two inch pipe, across the mouth of the shaft, held a set of ladders. The ladders hung close to the wall. Jargodin noted it would make a slow, careful trip up and down. Space would be at a minimum.

There were three more shafts on the claim all in a line and each had a corresponding pile of dirt beside it. Jargodin was absorbing it all as a car pulled up next to the caravan.

Three men got out. They each carried a small bag: they disappeared around the side of the van to where the door was situated. Jargodin sat and watched. They seemed a long time inside. Of course... he noted the port-gas bottle. They were having a cup of coffee... Confident miners.

Eventually they emerged. Each knew his respective task. One man put petrol in the generator and set it going: he checked the fuel level of the blower: he seemed satisfied. Two of the men had large plastic bags in their hands; that had to be the explosives and fuses. One man went down the ladders. There was a steel bell up top and tied to it a thin rope that went to the floor below. The rope jerked, the piece of steel hit another piece. The clang signalled the man below was ready. The man up top tied one of the bags on another rope and lowered it down. The process was repeated.

The man who had lowered the bags turned to his companion. There was a brief exchange of words then he too went down the ladders. Jargodin peering out from under his cap watched closely. He assumed their first job would be to connect the pipes on the floor below. Before blasting, the last two or three pipes closest to the face were disconnected and carried back out of the way of flying lumps of sandstone. The pipes would be re-connected, the blower started, and any explosive fumes sucked out. A clang on the steel knocker, signalled the man on top to start the blower. This was done. Gradually the revs were increased, then the familiar whine as dirt was fed into the pipes and sucked up into the hopper above.

The whine of the motor gave way to a steady beat. The man on top took hold of a rope tied to the flap under the hopper. When he thought the hopper was nearly full of dirt, he gave the rope a solid tug. The flap opened, the dirt fell on top of a mound already in the making. The day's work had begun.

Jargodin had seen enough. Sliding down the dump he made his way back to the car and headed home. He intended to return prior to knock off time.

CHAPTER. 19.

'What is going on?' Jargodin laughed. Paula, so intent on her work had not heard the arrival of the car. She looked up as Jargodin looked around the dug-out. Everything was pulled to the centre of the room. Buckets of water, a mop resting in one and Paula vigourously brandishing a broom up and down on the dug-out wall, told the story. No half measures. Their home was getting a spring cleaning from top to bottom.

'Ah, the hired help I rang for. You are just in time,' she said. She looked around, and with a wave of her hand she spoke. 'These walls have to be swept down, the floor has to be mopped out, all pieces of furniture has to be dusted and cleaned.' She stood there, barefooted, a brief pair of denim shorts, a small halter hoding back her breasts that threatened release. A smudge of dirt on her cheek and a line of sweat on her forehead gave her an impish look of innocence as she took in Jargodin's stunned look. He was equal to the occasion.

'Well, signora, I am only too happy to oblige, but first we must talk terms of my wages.'

'What would you suggest?'

'You are a beautiful woman. I would like to make love to you. Do you think your husband would mind?'

'Oh, no. He is out on the opal field somewhere. We could think about it when we finish.'

Jargodin walked slowly towards her. Their eyes were locked. 'Not after...now...right here on the floor.'

'On Madonna,' she whispered as her arms went around his neck.

Jesus, I was going back out to the field to check on that claim, ran through his mind: it wont matter if I am a bit late... This was to be regretted.

'What do you think?' she asked. They both stood back and looked around.

'I have to give you credit. It looks and smells clean and different. The improvement is amazing.'

'I can't take all the credit,' she laughed. 'The hired help made a big difference...his wages were a bit unusual.' Their happiness spilled over.

'Okay, listen darling, I want to do a quick trip out to the field. I should not be long: an hour at the outside.'

'Alright. I have a bit more to do here then I'll get cleaned up and get a meal on.' She gave him a quick kiss. 'Don't be long.'

It was after three o'clock. The fields were all but deserted. As he sped out to the fields he met only a few stragglers driving back in. He drove past the Sixteen mile turn off and continued to the edge of the Seventeen mile field: there he swung to the right and came into the Sixteen mile field from the rear. He pulled up between two large dumps. His car was hidden from view. Pick in hand he set off towards the Greek's claim.

What the hell am I doing here. I should have come out before all work had ceased. I knew I would be too late. I should have left it until tomorrow. I can't see anything of benefit now. I wanted to watch them come up to see if they were carrying opal. Go back home...come out again tomorrow. Ah, shit, I'm here now. I may as well have a look around. He pulled his cap down firmly on his head and like some irresistable magnet he was drawn towards the Greek's claim.

He stood beside a dump on the edge

of the claim. The field was deserted. He
wondered if they were getting opal. They
must be. Wait until Josef comes back.
We'll go down together one night. Get
out of here now. It seems a shame to be
out here and not know. They must have
blasted before knock off time. There
would still be fumes down below. There
are four shafts there creating a good
air flow. The fumes could all be gone.
Leave it! It is too bloody dangerous.
It's broad daylight. Come on, have some
sense. Ah, shit, there is no-one around.
I'll just have a quick look. There will
still be a few fumes so I'll go in, have
a look, and get out of the place. Jesus,
man, what would Paula say! Come on...a
quick glimpse...that wont hurt. He knew
he could not resist.

He walked swiftly over to the shaft,
swung on to the ladders and started
down.

Had Jargodin been there as he
intended and watched them finish their
day, he would have seen only two men
leave in the car instead of the three
that came. They had towed the caravan
there and decided that they would take
turns in camping on the field. They knew
of the robberies: they did not want to
be a victim. Sam, the youngest of the

three had been lying on the bunk in the caravan reading. He was thirsty. Getting off the bed he walked over to the sink where there were some bottles of mineral water. A small window over the sink made it possible to look out towards the blower and the rest of he claim.

It was a chance in a million. He looked out the window just as Jargodin was disappearing down the shaft. He just got a glimpse of the back of Jargodins shoulders. He could not believe his eyes... The realisation hit him... They were being robbed... in broad daylight.. Jesus! Unbelievable! Impossible!

A double-barrel shot-gun stood in the corner. He took two cartridges out of a drawer, loaded the gun and charged out over to the shaft. He looked down but could not see anything in the darkness below. Jargodin had already reached the bottom. He was standing in the drive his eyes adjusting to the semi-gloom.

'Bastard! You fucking bastard!' Sam screamed down the shaft. 'We've got you now, you thieving bastard,' He broke into a torrent of Greek, being able to express himself more vehemently in his mother tongue. He put down the shot-gun and bending over he grabbed the top rung of the set of six ladders. They hung suspended from the two inch pipe that stretched across the mouth of the shaft. Adrenalin pumping, he heaved the ladders, freeing the hooks from the pipe...He let the ladders drop.

As the bottom ladder hit the floor below and stopped, the rest kept coming as the hooks came free. The same process happened all the way up, creating a concertina effect. The result was that three ladders were criss-crossed at the base of the shaft, with the other three angled at intervals from halfway down.

'We've got you now you bastard! You can't get out! We'll fix you! There is a watchman not far away...I'll send him into town for the police. I'll just sit here with my gun...You're finished.' Sam screamed the words down into the darkness. Sam sped around the dumps to another caravan some four hundred metres away.

The startled watchman quickly grasped the situation and was soon on his way to town to notify the police and Sam's partners. Sam hurried back although confident the thief had no chance of escaping. He could not resist the temptation to gloat. He would be a hero.

'Oh, Christo,' Jargodin said. Who, how, where from? The questions hammered at his brain. 'Holy Mother of God, Paula!' Visions of his capture... Paula... Oh, shit, what a bloody mess. You fucking idiot. Take hold of yourself... calm down... steady, steady... Think.. Think.. There must have been someone in the caravan and they saw me. There is only one person. What did he say? Yes, that's right. Someone is going to town for the police. To town and back.. That gives me an hour, but how in the bloody hell am I going to get out. Steady now. There has to be a way.

He walked along the drive. Enough natural light came from the shafts for him to see. He walked to the shaft fartherest from the blower. He pictured the terrain above. There was a large dump of dirt between each shaft. If I can climb up the end shaft and keep that bastards attention at the main one.... A smile broke through his sombre thoughts. He hurried back.

He surveyed the tangled ladders. One of them with a bit of pushing and shoving could be easily taken out. He set to, keeping his body back in the drive with only his arm reaching out into the shaft. There was a lot of clanging against the pipes as he freed the ladder.

Sam heard the noise below. He leant over peering down but could see nothing. What the hell was going on?

Jargodin looked up from the rim of the shaft. The top half of Sam's body was clearly outlined against the sky. I've got to keep you there you bastard, was Jargodin's main concern.

All the necessary tools and equipment for mining were stacked against the nearby wall. Jargodin grabbed one of the picks and a roll of fuse. He still had his own small pick pushed through his belt.

He wrapped four half hitches of the fuse around the galvanised pipe a metre off the ground. He then wrapped another four half hitches tightly around the end of the handle of the pick so it hung suspended. He played the fuse down the length of the handle to the pick head and there wrapped some more half hitches around the pick and head of the handle. He played out a length of fuse and gave it a tug. The pick pulled back and when he released the fuse it hit the hollow pipe sending a vibrating ring up to the top. It worked well. He gave a few more tugs. The noise was loud and clear.

Jargodin picked up the steel ladder he had freed and ran back to the last shaft. He stood it upright so that the top few rungs went up the neck of the shaft. He now went back for the roll of fuse and played it out behind as once more he went back to the last shaft. He gave the fuse a few more tugs. The noise echoed again. He nodded. He would have to tug the fuse at intervals to keep the Greek's attention back where he was.

Sammy was confused. What was the bastard doing down there? What was the noise? It was something hitting the pipes, but what? What was he up to? He would have to stay there and wait. Never mind, we've got him trapped... Clang, clang! What is going on?

Jargodin set the ladder as close to the vertical as he dared, so it would not bend as he climbed. Jesus mate, you are going to be tested now. Paula...uh...no way...you can't think of anything else but the job on hand...put everything else out of your mind. He took a deep breath and picked up the remaining roll of fuse...it would have to go with him..He put it inside his shirt, tightened his belt and started to climb the ladder.

His head and shoulders were inside the neck of the shaft. He examined the walls. This was the crucial part...He had to dig two holes in the wall to accomodate the ends of the ladder. They had to be far enough up the side of the wall and in deep enough so the ground below was stong enough to hold his weight and not give way, otherwise...he didn't want to think what might happen.,

His actions were careful and deliberate. He took his small pick from his belt and with careful balance started to dig...Sweat broke out on his brow...it required exact muscle control. He steadily picked out two holes. He had carefully measured the width of the ladder with his hand span, doing the same on the wall. It was important to get the holes the right distance apart on the first attempt.

The holes had to have enough angle up the wall so the ladder could slope upwards...Madre Mio, I think it is okay. 'Here goes,' he muttered. This was going to take some doing.

He pushed his pick back inside his belt. He would need to get further up into the shaft. He would have to go one rung higher. He lifted one leg on to a higher rung and with every bit of control in his body put his weight on it and brought the other leg up. Slowly, ever so slowly, he straightened, his hands going out to the sides of the shaft to try and balance.

Keep going, you can't stop and rest... Keep going. Turning on an angle, he spread his arms wide against the wall. With elbows bent slightly to gain better purchase, he carefully lifted one leg off the ladder extending it out in front to the opposite side. Tensing he pushed hard in all directions. With his shoulders pressed backwards and his foot pushing hard against the other side, he jammed his body. It was hot. The sweat pored down his face. Carefully he released the weight off his other foot on the ladder and lifted his leg up beside the other. He made it and locked all positions. He gave a sigh of relief, put his hand inside his shirt and gave the fuse two more tugs.

Takintg out his pick, he hooked it under the top rung of the ladder and lifted it up; when it was within reach he grabbed the ladder with his free hand. He re-adjusted his hold and slid the ladder upwards until the bottom legs could be moved into the holes on the wall. It was strenuous, exacting work.

His body was a lather of perspiration. The ladder legs fitted comfortably into the holes . The ladder was now angled up against the opposing wall. Two more tugs on the fuse. Would the ground below the holes hold?

He crabbed his body around and up. He reached out and grasped the ladder. There was no other choice. He had to get his body around. He freed one foot from the wall and moved his leg around. He got his foot on the bottom rung. It was the moment of truth. He worked himself around. Both feet were on the rung...it held. Still holding his small pick in one hand he climbed the rungs. Half way up the ladder, it bowed slightly...a stab of fear ran through him. He climbed a further two rungs. Everything was okay.

Oh, shit. This is tough, but, I've got to win...He thought of Paula. I've got to win. He started once again to dig two more holes. The first part was the hardest. He grew confident knowing if he kept his head, he could do it. He wasn't wearing a watch so he didn't have any idea how long he had been there. It seemed like an eternity, but common sense told him it was perhaps ten minutes at the outside.

He went through the same proceedure. This time he was much quicker and it was less strenuous. He repeated it again and again. He looked up. The mouth of the shaft above beckoning him, still seemed a long way off. Time was passing. He increased his pace slightly but did not for one second relax his concentration. The circus had taught him well.

My God, he thought. I am almost there. One more set of holes. Don't get over confident. He still continued to give the ever decreasing roll of fuse a tug. Thank God, there was nearly a full roll.

He dug the two remaining holes and with a final effort soon had the ladder in position. It was the last climb. The top of the ladder almost reached the top of a pile of loose dirt around the hole.

He cept up the ladder. Careful, don't stuff everything up now. A feeling of elation came over him as he looked around. The large sandstone dumps were between him and Sam. He scrambled over the top. Holy bloody hell. I've made it. Let me get to hell out of here. He took the roll of fuse out of his shirt. He gave it several quick final tugs then dropped the roll on the ground. Leave everything...Get going!

Crouched over, he sped out and around, making sure to keep the large heaps between him and the Greek's claim. Oh, Jesus, I made it! He wasted no time in getting back to his car. He drove back out of the sixteen mile field on to the main road back to town. He turned off the road and pulled over beside some old workings. He was safe. He took a packet of cigarettes out of the glove box. His hands shook as he fumbled with the packet. Re-action set in...Jesus, I never want to go through that again...Oh, shit, Paula will kill me. What do I tell her?

Oh, Jesus, that was a bloody nightmare. No more of that...how bloody stupid can a bloke get...Madre Mio!

From where he sat he had a clear view of the road and the track across to the Sixteen mile field. He did not want to be driving back to town and run into the Police and Sam's partners coming out. He wasn't sure of the time element, but knew they should soon be coming into view.

He had not long to wait. Speeding vehicles followed by trails of dust were only a few kilometres away. He watched as they left the main road and sped across the open space to the Sixteen mile. Two four wheel drives followed by two cars made up the contingement. Jargodin laughed to himself. Sorry you bastards, the bird has flown. Madonna! I can imagine their surprise. Jargodin waited until they had disappeared fron view as they entered the workings. He started his car and drove back to the safety of his dug-out.

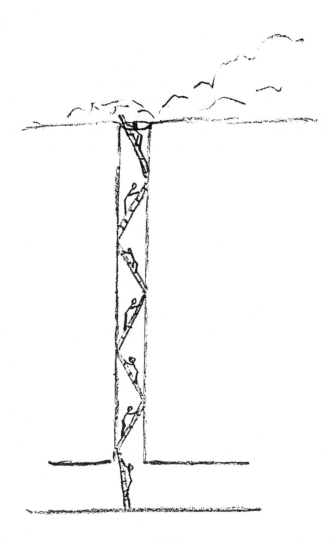

CHAPTER. 20.

Sam was getting worried. No noise had come from below for some time. What the hell was going on down there? He couldn't understand it..something queer had happened. He looked at his watch. They should be coming out from town soon. He glanced back towrds the road. Billows of dust could be seen above the mulloch heaps.

As he watched, fresh clouds, coming towards him, rose skywards. He listened. The sound of vehicles came to his ears. At last..

Sam was gesticulating wildly, as typically, in rapid fire Greek he explained to his partners, what had happened. The police sergeant and a constable, together with two men from the mines department, stood patiently waiting.

With gestures, and reverting to English, the story unfolded. He saw the guy go down the hole. No, he couldn't recognise him. He only saw the back of his head and shoulders. Yes, of course he is still down there. How in the bloody hell could he get out. Yes, I dropped the ladders down the shaft, then went to get this chap. He pointed to the chap from the other caravan who had also arrived on the scene. No, the bloke down below never said a word. All I heard was noises. What sort of noises? Noises...like knocking. Where? Where do you think?..Down there..Down the bottom of this shaft. No, I haven't heard any noises for a while, but he is still there...Sam laughed...Don't worry. I have caught the bastard..His chest swelled with pride.

The mines warden turned to George the oldest of the Greeks. 'George can you get another set of ladders We will drop them down this other shaft.' He pointed to the nearby shaft. 'Then start your generator. We will need some lights down below. I'll yell out from up here explaining the situation. He will have to come up.'

'I go down and get the bastard Syd. If he no come up. I take the gun,' he pointed to the shot-gun. 'He come up, but, maybe dead.'

'Nothing like that I'm afraid George. You get the ladders and get some lights going. I'll have a look around,' the Sergeant said. The Greeks hurried to borrow a set of ladders from a neighbouring claim. Sergeant Neil walked away.

All was in readiness. A set of ladders had been lowered down the shaft. The generator was going and lights were on underground. Sergeant Neil wandered back. 'I don't think you will find anyone down there,' he said.

They all looked at him. 'What do you mean! He is down there. I saw him go down. He has to be there!' Sammy said angrily.

The Sergeant shook his head. 'I am afraid not. While you were here watching this hole, he climbed out of the end one. With these mounds of dirt,' the Sergeant's fingers pointed to the dumps, 'you couldn't see what was happening down further.'

This was received with stunned silence, followed by a tirade of Greek from George, aimed at Sammy. They hurried around to the last shaft. The ladder lay as Jargodin had left it, it's position all too revealing.

Syd Slart, the mining warden, looked in amazement. 'I'll be buggered,' he said, as he shook his head.

Descending the ladders, the story was revealed. Sammy's partners turned on him and in a mixture of Greek and English called him the biggest idiot of all time.

The bush telegraph soon spread the story. Sammy's humiliation was complete. He was the butt of innumerable jokes. One prankster had the audacity to put a slip of paper on a communal notice board reading..'Wanted, position of night watchman. Sammy.' Sammy would have easily strangled the culprit were he to be found.

Syd Slart and Sergeant Neil stood apart talking, as order in the claim was being restored.'No ordinary thief this one,' Syd said.

Sergeant Neil looked at the mines warden. 'You can say that again. He's got brains as well as guts although it was bloody stupid, going down in the middle of the afternoon. That was a stroke of genius that pick business, but, you would have to be a bloody acrobat to get up that shaft the way he did.'

'That is for sure. You would need circus training...Oh, shit, no.' The impact of Syd's words hit them both at the same time. 'Oh, Jesus, no. Couldn't be.

Sergeant Neil shook his head slowly.

'In this job...I am never surprised..Could be. Look, don't say a word of this to anyone. We could quite easily ruin a reputation here and that is the last thing we want. It could be one of a number on this field. Gawd knows, there are that many people of so many different nationalities we don't know who we have living here. If the truth is known, we probably have some of the best thieves in the world hiding here.'

'Yes, I guess you are right. It was my saying, circus, that brought us both to think as we did.'

'Yes, let's forget it Syd. Looks like we may have a real professional on our hands, but, I think he will lay low after this close shave.'

'I hope the bastard leaves town.

CHAPTER. 21.

Word of the bizaree escapade spread like wild fire. A town without television and poor radio reception, word of mouth, was the main news source. Distorted and exagerated versions were being traded in the hotel and the clubs. The tales lost none of their drama in the telling, and, of course, hundreds of thousands of dollars worth of opal was taken!

The inevitable happened. A few just happened to mention, that, whoever was responsible had to be a 'bloody acrobat.' This statement, although said accidentially, brought only one name to mind. Unlike the sergeant of police and the mines warden, who with discretion, kept their views to themselves, Jargodin's name was freely mentioned.

With no evidence against him, Jargodin was the culprit and as the tales grew, all other robberies were laid at his door step. He became known as, 'The Moonlighter.'

To his fellow countrymen he was a hero. The Australian miners with the hero worship of Ned Kelly bred in their veins, laughed and saluted his daring. No Australian miner had been robbed so far: as long as that remained the 'status quo,' everything would be okay. Some members of the community were outraged. They feared what it might lead to...they had good reason for their fear...Coober Pedy, would never be the same again.

Jargodin became known to all and sundry overnight. He was loved, hated, and admired, but he could not be denied. As he walked, his footsteps echoed the excitement of being alive.

It was two days since the event. Jargodin was in a quandry. He wanted to tell Paula, but was ashamed to do so. He cursed himself for being, 'so bloody stupid.' He had put everything in jeopardy...worst of all, he had nearly brought shame to Paula. What to do? Tell her...he wanted to...maybe nothing will be said....

They had worked on the dug-out, cleaning, scrubbing, painting and re-arranging. The change was miraculous. they both looked at it with pride. Could he go straight...take the risk? Paula's family!...He knew time was limited...there was only one way...A few more quick jobs and then run...He needed more money...Maybe they had enough now...

He sat nursing a cup of coffee. Paula had taken the car and gone to the supermarket. They needed groceries. He sat in trepidation awaiting her return. He will have to tell her. He owes her that. He heard the car door slam and knew he was in trouble. 'Jargodin! You bastard! You 'testa dura,' you...you...Oh, Madonna what have you done,' she wailed. She stood there, pale and trembling a mixture of emotions, not knwing whether to cry or scream in rage. 'Oh, shit...I don't know what to think.' She walked to the table and sat down.

Her indignation and rage took over. Her elbows on the table she leant towards him. 'You know that old crony, with the missing teeth...Duschin's wife darling,' she gritted. 'The one you, jumped inside out for.' Jargodin nodded.

'Yes, nod you stupido. 'Eh, Paula,' she says to me. 'That man of yours, Jargodin, he been busy eh? He fix up those Greek fellas good eh?' I didn't know what the hell she was talking about.

'By gee, he game that Jargodin. He make them fool eh? He make plenty money too eh?' Well, by this time my warning bells are ringing.

I laughed. 'Oh, sure, he fix them up, but maybe you didn't hear the truth. You tell me what you heard.' Well she told me. I was amazed as well as disgusted, but I had to cover you. Didn't I darling?' she hissed. 'So, my precious one, I laughed at the old dear. No way, I said. We have been painting the dug-out. Jargodin has not been out for two days. Must be someone else and Jargodin gets the blame. This threw the old girl. Anyhow I left. Now you supid idiot, tell me the truth!' She pommelled the table with her fists. It was all too much. She broke down and cried.

She wasn't finished. She lifted her head and wiped her eyes. The fire came back into her once more. 'The great Jargodin. In the middle of the afternoon...the middle of the afternoon mind you...The star of the circus...The great escape artist..., shit, you should have been a bloody clown.' The tears came again.

Jargodin sat and watched. He felt so hopeless. My God, I love her. Please don't leave me. What a fool I've been. No more...We have enough money...We'll go..We'll leave...As soon as Johnny has our passports we'll go.

He walked around and knelt by her chair. He reached out and took her hand. 'Paula,' he said gently. 'Look at me.' She turned her tear-stained face towards him. 'I'm sorry. I'll explain. No-one knows that it was me, but, before we go any further...No more...There will be no more. We have enough money. We have well over a hundred thousand dollars. As soon as· Johnny gets our passports we will go...No more thieving...I promise...I love you Paula...You are my whole world...please don't leave me...Without you I am nothing.'

'You mean it, Jargodin, you really mean it...no more?'

'Sure sweetheart...No more.' He stood up and helped her to her feet. 'You are beautiful. I love you.'

'On, God, I must look a mess,' she laughed as she put her arms around his neck.

'That is the truth. I knew it was a stupid thing to do, but, I couldn't resist the challenge.'

She shook her head in amazement. 'Holy Maria! Incredible. How you got away is unbelievable. Oh God, if you had got caught...I Don't know what I would have done. I have defied my family, the Mafia and everything for you...' As if talking to herself, she continued. 'Up home, certain times of the year, plain turkeys, or bustards as they are known, would come down around our place. An old aboriginal chap told me, that they would mate for life. If anything happened to one of them, the other never took on another partner.' She looked steadily at Jargodin. 'I guess I would be like those plain turkeys...please, no more Jargodin. It does not sit easy with me. I guess generations of it being bred in me made it posible for me to accept, but thank God, it is all over.' Her mood changed, a giggle escaped her lips.

'I would loved to have seen their faces when they discovered the bird had flown.' They both laughed. Everything was okay.

'Well, I guess life will be boring now,' he gave a wry grin.

'Don't count on it my darling, I have this funny inbuilt system that says, there is a lot more drama to come. Oh hell, I forgot. When I went down town, I bumped into Josef. He had just arrived back from Adelaide. I invited him around for chicken and spaghetti. With all this other business it completely slipped my mind. I had best get busy.'

Josef's arrival with a bottle of wine, set a pleasant atmosphere that carried throughout the meal. They sat around the table comfortable with each other, sipping coffee.

'I didn't want to say anything before, as it could have upset your appetites...Tom Tom died today.'

'What! Poor bastard. Oh, hell, I liked the guy. I was only speaking to him a couple of days ago.'

Josef nodded. 'Yes, apparently he collapsed in the pub, only acouple of hours ago. They took him to the hospital, but he was dead on arrival.'

'Who was Tom Tom, Jargodin?' Paula asked.

'You know him. He was always with the aborigines. He lived with a gin. He had a dug-out down on the flat. A skinny white guy. Always had a cigarette holder in his mouth, with or without a cigarette. The aborigines would clean up the opal they got and Tom Tom would flog it around the pub for them.

'He's been here for years. He worked for some government department up in Darwin as a gardener before he came here. They had to put him on a pension. He was too sick to work. I think he was only supposed to live for six months when he came here.

'He has collapsed untold times in the pub. I don't think he has eaten a square meal in years. He has lived on plonk and cigarettes. The old gin he has shacked up with wouldn't be capable of cooking a meal. I think Tom Tom used to cook up the occasional pot of stew and that with salami and cheese was the diet.

'Poor bastard. What happens now Josef?'

'Well, the normal thing here is they have to be buried the next day. There is no freezing chambers here, only a cool room. The heat being excessive here, the bodies go off quickly. We usually go up to the hospital in our cars. The police come up in their station wagon. The coffin is put in the station wagon and is taken out to the cemetry. At least he will be in the new cemetry at 'Boot

Hill.' A lot of the guys usually wait in the pub until they see the station wagon coming then they join the tail. Only a few of the guys go to the hospital.'

'Bloody hell. I'll go up to the hospital in the morning. I'll get there early in case his gin is there. Maybe I can help with a few dollars.'

'You don't have to worry about funeral costs. The Government buries them.'

'Yeah, I know, but I may be able to do something,' Jargodin said.

The hospital was a low slung wooden building and the mortuary was in the back at the base of the hill. A few stunted trees helped keep it from view. A young nurse, a big raw-boned country lass, plodded her way down to the building. She didn't like this side of nursing. They were short staffed. She was sent to dress the body. She was not used to death. It was spooky being down there alone.

Opening the door, she paused, willing herself to master her fear. She fumbled for the light switch and pushed it on. The cool air inside should have been a relief from the morning heat, but it wasn't. The cool clinical smell and stillness didn't help her. She shivered.

Large trays, like a chest of drawers, slid into the wall. She grasped the handles of the one containing Tom Tom's body and sharply pulled it out.

Tom Tom sat up. He was wild-eyed and staring. A hospital gown was draped over his thin frame. 'I'm cold,' he screeched. 'I'm cold. Where's my bloody clothes? They're trying to kill me. Let me out.' He started to scramble out of his tomb as he ranted.

The nurse gave one piercing scream and fled out the door. She could be heard screeching as she headed up the path, 'Matron, Matron!'

Tom Tom wasted no time fleeing from his nightmare. He scarpered outside with just the thin white gown clutched around him. He fled up a path beside the hospital that led to the road beside the main entrance.

He glanced wildly around. Amazingly, fifty metres away, sat old Charlie the aborigine, in the car Jargodin had bought him. When later asked why he was there and so early, Charlie shrugged. It still amazes the so called intellectuals, the telephatic powers of the aboriginee race. Charlie said, 'he knew to be there.' That was it...no great mystery...He could not understand what all the fuss was about. Charlie, however, did not bargain on what was to happen.

Tom Tom spotted Charlie. Salvation...With his gown now flapping loosely around him, he looked like Ghandi in full flight as he sped to Charlie and his car.

Charlie had been staring ahead, his mind blank. The passenger door being wrenched open and then slammed shut made him turn and look. There was the spectre of Tom Tom. 'Take me home Charlie! Take me home!' Tom Tom screamed. 'They're all mad here. Mad! They're mad!'

Charlies eyes opened wide...his mouth fell open...a long drawn out wail came out of his mouth...'Aaaaah...You dead...aaah, you dead.' Charlies gaunt frame shook from head to toe.

Tom Tom, still frantic from his experience stared at Charlie. 'What the fuck you talk about Charlie. I'm alive,' he screamed. 'Here, feel me. I'm alive.' He extended his hand to Charlie to feel.

'Aaaah,' it was the last straw for Charlie. He opened his door, and leaving it ajar fled. Charlie had not run so fast since the days of his youth in the Pitjatjinjarra country chasing kangaroo. Arms waving and uttering incoherent cries, he headed for the aborigine camp.

'Shit, what's the matter with him. They have all gone mad,' Tom Tom said, as he scrambled out of the seat.

At this very moment, Jargodin, arriving early, drove up to the hospital. Tom Tom recognised Jargodin and his car as he came towards him. He had to stop him. Flapping his arms up and down for Jargodin to stop, he stood in the middle of the road.

Jargodin stared at this weird ghost like figure in white in front of him, waving his arms. 'What the fucking hell is going on,' he said to himself. 'Shit, it's Tom Tom!' Jargodin had now stopped a few metres from Tom Tom who had run around to the passenger's side. He opened the door and climbed in.

Jargodin stared at him in astonishment. 'What the fucking hell is going on. You're supposed to be dead. You nearly gave me a heart attack. I'm still not too sure whether this is real or not.... You are alive aren't you? What are you doing running around the street in that fucking fancy dress?'

'Of course I'm alive you stupid bastard. They tried to kill me there. They were going to bury me alive. Take me home! Quick Jargodin, take me home before they put me back in that fucking morgue!'

Without realising it and bowing to Tom Tom's urgency, Jargodin had turned the car around and was driving back towards town. He went to pull over on the side of the road to sort things out.

'No, no. Keep going take me back to my dug-out. Quick. Jesus, give me a cigarette will you?'

Jargodin swung back on to the road and increased the speed. It was all too much for Jargodin. He started to laugh. 'Here, for God's sake have a smoke.' He passed his cigarettes and matches across. 'Keep them. Your need is greater than mine. I'll take you home, but, shit, tell me what happened. Everybody is getting ready to go to your funeral. Oh, Jesus.' Tears of laughter came to his eyes as he shook his head from side to side. 'Oh, Jesus, how priceless!'

'They aren't going to my funeral! No way! I'm not going to die for those bastards! I was drinking at the pub and I must have passed out. The next thing I know, I'm in a fucking tomb. It's dark and I can't move. They have taken my clothes off and I have got this fucking gown on me. I can't get out! The top is only centimetres above my face. Oh, shit, I thought I must be buried already. They've buried me the bastards, I thought.

'I nearly went crazy. I shouted and screamed and nothing happened. Anyhow, I must have passed out again. The next thing I know, this nurse pulls me out and here I am in this bloody drawer. It was bloody cold.

'I up and off. I came outside and old Charlie was there in his car. I jumped in beside him, and, he got out and took off for his life!

Jargodin had been chuckling quietly to himself but he couldn't restrain himself any longer. He burst into uncontrolled laughter.

'So, they don't know at the hospital where you are?'

'No. Stuff them. I'm going home. I'll put some clothes on and go down to the pub.'

'Yes, but don't you think you should tell them at the hospital. You should see the doctor.' 'What!' Tom Tom exploded. 'That's the bastard who said I was dead. He wants to bury me! No way! You see I have this problem with my pulse. I don't know what they call it, but at the best of times, you are flat out finding my pulse. No way. I'm not going back there.'

'Oh, God, I've seen and heard everything now. Okay we are nearly back to your place. You get dressed and I'll take you back to the hospital. Okay?'

'No. Wait for me while I get dressed, then I'll get a ride down town to the pub.' Jargodin shrugged as he turned into a dead-end and Tom Tom's dug-out.

A litter of empty tins and cartons, a couple of mangy dogs lying in the dust, and four lubras sitting up against the sandstone wall, greeted them as Jargodin pulled up. The gins were wailing and rolling about. Tom Tom's gin had curt her head with rocks. Trickles of blood mixed with dust ran down her face.

'Look at the stupid bitches,' he said, even though he knew it was for him they were lamenting. He got out of the car and walked up to them.

'What do you think you're doing, you stupid bloody things?'

The wailing stopped immediately. The silence was deafening...All of a sudden, all hell broke loose. The gins all bar Tom Tom's woman, took off. They, like old Charlie, recaptured their youthful agility and last seen were screeching their way back to town, determined to shake off the ghost they had just seen.

Tom Tom's woman fell back in a dead faint. Her dress, her only garment, had come up around her waist revealing her skinny legs, crutch and bony thighs.

'Pull your dress down you silly woman. How many times have I got to tell you.' He reached down and yanked her dress down. Just then she came to...sat up...her head wobbled around and her eyes focussed on Tom Tom...She passed out again. Tom Tom shook his head in disgust and walked inside.

In a matter of minutes, Tom Tom was back out dressed. He had thrown water on his face and run a comb through his sparse hair. A shirt that once was white, an old pair of trousers and barefooted, Tom Tom was dressed for town.

He had a half full flagon of wine in his hand. His woman was now showing signs of coming back to reality. She was leaning against the wall as he shook her shoulder. 'Here, woman. You have a drink. I'm going down town for a while.' She was like a rubber zombie that had no control of its body.

Her head lolled from side to side, her eyes glazed and her open mouth drooled saliva. She looked at him in a mixture of terror and bewilderment.'Aaaah,' she said and passed out once more.

Tom Tom shrugged and muttering to himself walked to the car and got in the front seat. 'Bloody women,' he said.

Jargodin was still suppressing laughter as he let Tom Tom out in front of the hotel. Pointing to the pub, he said, 'A lot of your fans are in there Tom Tom. You are sure going to create a storm.' Putting his hand in his pocket, he pulled out a few notes and thrust them into Tom Tom's hand. 'It isn't every day I go to a funeral and end up driving the body back to the pub for a drink. Good luck.' He reached across and opened Tom Tom's door for him.

'You know, Tom Tom, you could make a lot of money out of this. You could claim to be the new Messiah...risen from the dead.'

Jargodin was still laughing to himself as he drove back home. Wait till I tell Paula!

CHAPTER. 022.

Blowers, mounted on trucks, whined as they sucked the dirt up from underground and spewed a continual stream of fine dust into the atmosphere. New dumps were being formed in front of their eyes, as the hoppers opened their doors and the discarded rubble dropped and spread. Noodlers stood back. When the fresh load of dirt dropped, they quickly moved in searching for pieces of opal.

The subdued thumps of eplosives told of another 'face,' being blown underground. York hoists rattled as they pulled up the fifty litre buckets of dirt. The field was a hive of activity.

Paula, Josef and Jargodin, had come out for a look around. Paula and Jargodin both were carefree and relaxed since the decision of,'no more.' It showed in their faces. They stood gazing about. 'Incredible, isn't it? A sight like this will probably never be seen again. It would have to be one of the richest fields ever.' Paula turned to him as he spoke.

She nodded. 'It is quite breath taking. Come on let's walk.'

They meandered around the claims. Nick, a middle aged Greek had just emptied a bucket of dirt on the perimeter of his mound as they approached. He glared at Jargodin as he neared and spat contemptuously on the ground in his direction. The insult was obvious. Jargodin stopped. Paula was shocked. She took Jargodin's arm.

'Come on Jargodin. Ignore him.'

Jargodin shook his head. 'No, don't move. Just stand here. Don't do a thing.' The three of them stopped. Nick put the empty bucket back on the hook. He swung the arm of the York hoist over the shaft and controlling the break let the bucket down. A few seconds later a clang on his bell signalled him to start hauling. The motor groaned under the pressure as the wire started to rewind. Eventually another full bucket of dirt came into view. Nick swung the loaded bucket around from the shaft and let it fall once more on the edge of the dump.

Nick had expected them to keep walking. He shot a quick glance in their direction. As he emptied the bucket he muttered a few words.

'I don't think they were compliments,' Josef said.

'Jargodin. Come on. Leave him be. Who is he anyway?' Paula asked.

'Who is he?' Jargodin's raised voice made sure Nick could hear every word. 'Look at the peasant bastard. He's supposed to be one of the richest men on the field. Just get a look at him.'

It was common knowledge that Nick owned flats and houses in Adelaide, yet dressed and lived like a peasant. An old ill-fitting pair of trousers, held up with a tie for a belt that was knotted under an over-hanging stomach. A old pair of army boots split at the sides and laced with a piece of string, should have been given a military funeral... they had seen so much active service. A torn short sleeve flannel shirt, a cap revealing tufts of grey hair protruding above his ears and a moustache that drooped in sympathy with a turned down mouth, was what they saw.

'Jargodin, come on! Let's go.'

'Just a little bit longer,' Jargodin chuckled.

Nick, now starting to feel uncomfortable with the scrutiny, kept working. He didn't know how to cope with the situation. Another bucket was coming up.

'Josef, just look at that.' Jargodin's voice was once again raised. 'He takes all day to bring up a bucket. That poor bloke underground must sit down and have a cigarette while he waits for the next bucket. I tell you what Josef, I'll bet I could climb up a rope from below, faster than he can pull a bucket of dirt up with the winch.'

Josef was quick to catch on. Ah,...I don't know...No matter how slow he is, to climb up a rope would take some time...that is...if you could climb up a rope from down there.'

'No problem, I'll bet I could climb up a rope faster than that old bastard could pull up a bucket of dirt.'

One thing Nick was not, was a wimp...To be called an old bastard was too much. What Jargodin didn't know was that the claim he went down that afternoon was financed by Nick. He was a partner and he like a lot of people believed Jargodin to be the guilty one. His humiliation over the episode was deep.

He emptied the bucket of dirt stood up and glared at Jargodin. 'You a no good theiving basta...All talk...all bullshit...never mind talk..put money up.' Nick had let his anger take over.

Jargodin paused as if to think about it...'They tell me you are a very mean man. If, I win, maybe you would not pay me.'

The insult hit home. The Greeks on the field were heavy gamblers. Nick was no exception. He always carried money with him. You never knew when some mining machinery was going cheap. He put his hand deep into his pocket and pulled out a roll of fifty dollar bills. He peeled off ten and waved them at Jargodin. 'Five hundred dollars. Where's your money?' he chortled.

Jargodin shrugged and pulled out a roll of equal proportion. He counted off ten and held them up. 'Here's my money.'

'Oh, Madonna,' Paula crossed herself as she spoke. She turned to Josef. 'What am I going to do with this man. We come for a walk around and this...this has to happen.'

Josef laughed. 'Don't worry. Everything will be okay. If he hadn't spat at us, there would have been no problem. You can't let him get away with that.'

She shook her head in resignation and gave a low laugh. 'Okay, I hate peace. What happens now?'

A few miners nearby had been watching and now strolled over. At the sight of the money being waved around, some had called out to their mates. Josef went back to the car for Jargodin's rope. By the time he returned, the bush telegraph had done it's job and a small crowd had collected.

There was an atmosphere of a serious challenge...it was a biased Greek showing his contempt for a rogue Croation and visa-versa.

Len Butts, a popular figure on the field, came on the scene and was soon told about the wager. Len a happy go lucky extrovert took charge.

'Nick, I'll be referee. Okay by you? I'll handle the money.' Nick wondered at how the hell all this had happened, but he would show that bastard. 'Yes, no worries Len.' Len turned to Jargodin, winking at him as he did so. 'Okay by you Jargodin?'

Jargodin laughed. 'Go ahead Len. Here is my $500. Make sure you get his.'

The crowd had grown. A group of aboriginals noodling nearby, had now joined the crowd that had swelled alarmingly. Len picked up a stick and drew a line in the sand. A carnival atmosphere had taken over. 'Right, everybody, now listen. Nick has given me $500 dollars and so has Jargodin. Those who want to back Nick, I'll put your money this side of the line, and those who want to back Jargodin, your money will be this side of the line.'

'What's it all about?' came a voice from the rear. 'We've just arrived.'

Len looked over towards where the voice came from. 'Okay I'll tell you once only. Jargodin said he can come up a rope from underground, faster than Nick can pull a full bucket of dirt up. Now if Nick loses any of the dirt by hitting the sides, he loses the bet. Josef has put a pipe across this shaft here which is only five metres away from the one Nick is using. They are the same depth. I will give the signal to start. Nick will then start his motor and pull away and Jargodin will start climbing. I will stand at the edge of Jargodin's shaft so he will be able to see my hand drop. Okay, place your bets.'

A buzz of talk and laughter swept through the crowd.

'Heh, Nick,' a voice called out. 'There is someone singing out from down below.' Everybody listened and a voice could be plainly heard. Nick gave a startled cry, ran to the winch, and started the motor. 'Oh, Jesus, he's forgotten his partner,' someone said. The crowd laughed.

Another Greek miner standing near Jargodin spoke. 'The silly bastard forgot all about Sam. Actually his partner is sick today so he got his nephew to give him a hand. I don't know why he didn't have a day off himself. God knows he doesn't need the money. I'm not having a bet, but I hope you take his money... but, man,... to back yourself coming up a rope against a winch....?' he slowly shook his head.

A head and shoulders emerged from Nick's shaft, then the whole figure emerged on the narrow seat used for riding up and down. Joef gave a groan. 'Oh, shit. That Sammy is the one who spotted you going down the shaft,' he whispered to Jargodin.

'Great,' Jargodin said. 'I hope he has a bet.' He looked at Josef. 'You going to have a bet?'

'That is for bloody sure.'

'Good, well wait until we see if Sammy bets. If he does, cover him. Okay?'

'No problem.

Sam looked in amazement at the crowd that had gathered. He looked to Nick for an answer. There was a quick tirade of Greek, with much gesturing and pointing. Sam couldn't believe this was happening. He looked at Jargodin...the one who had made a fool of him...his eyes blazed. He had no choice.

In an over dramatised, theatrical childish manner, he spat on the ground, puffed out his chest and slowly walked over to Lennie. From his jeans he also took a roll of notes. 'I bet three hundred dollars against that one.' He scornfully indicated Jargodin with his head. Everyone was watching and listening.

Josef quickly stepped forward. 'I cover that bet.' The talk resumed in earnest. Comments rolled back and forth. Different ones walked up to Len with varying amounts. He was busy setting one against the other.

'I've got two hundred here backing the winch that I haven't covered. Anybody take it, or part of it.'

'Mine Len. I'll take it.' Len looked up at the speaker.

'Ok, Lovro, yours. No sweat.' His hand reached out for the money.

'Impossible... nobody can beat a winch.'

'I'll back Jargodin for fifty.'

'This bloody Jargodin will go up that fast, you wait and see. I've watched him.'

'Don't be ridiculous. You ever tried climbing up a rope out of a shaft. I can tell you, it is hard work. I know, I've done it. The winch will be up, hours before Jargodin.'

'Jeez, this is stupid. Nobody can beat a winch. Twenty on the winch.'

'Stuff it, I don't like the bastard. I'll back Jargodin even if I do my money.'

'Yeah, but don't forget, if you pull too fast and the bucket goes off centre, it will start bouncing against the sides and you will lose the dirt.' Back and forth, for and against, the opinions intermingled.

A shrill voice rose above the rest. Rosy, pushed her large aboriginal frame forward. 'Hey Lennie,' she grinned. 'I back that Jargodin fella. Hey Jargodin!' She turned to Jargodin, who, eyes twinkling, grinned back at her. 'You no gammon eh? You fella come up rope like goanna up tree eh?'

'Don't you worry, Rosy, You my number two girl next to Paula here. I never tell you gammon.'

'Aieee,' chortled Rosy. There was laughter all around. She thrust a handful of creased notes into Lennies hand. 'I back 'im Jargodin.'

Paula stood there taking it all in...it's unbelievable...unreal...she shook her head. 'Where else in the world,' she thought, . 'could such a thing happen?'

To Jargodin, this was a serious challenge. The gymnastic effort required represented a part of his past that was sacred to him. He withdrew into himself. 'See it in your mind...not once...not twice, but over and over again. It must be done in your mind first.' Dolfoes words rang loud and clear.

More people had arrived. Work had virtually stopped. What had started as an insult had escalated into a rare and unusual event.
there was now over four thousand dollars being bet. It was talked about for years to come, it was, as someone said, 'unbelievable.' Silence had descended. Sammy had gone below and filled the bucket with dirt. It now rested at the bottom of the shaft. The slack had been taken in the wire. The winch motor was silent.

Jargodin, his hands on his rope

stood at the bottom of the adjacent shaft. He was breathing deeply, his mind concentrated on the climb.

The crowd softly shuffled about seeking the best view. Their eyes were glued to the two gaping mouths of the shafts.

Len stood at the edge of Jargodin's shaft. He leant over slightly so Jargodin could, as well as hear his voice, see his hand, holding a handkerchief, drop. He looked down into Jargodin's upturned face.

Most of Jargodin's backers, didn't think he could beat the winch. It was mainly Croation money against Greek money. Factional hatred had reared its ugly head.

Paula stood, white faced and tense. Josef standing beside her seemed quite composed. He squeezed Paula's arm and whispered, 'don't worry. He'll win.' She gave him a sickly, although thankful smile. 'Go!' Lennies hand dropped as he yelled. Nick's motor burst into life. This was the crucial part for Nick. If he jerked the bucket too fast, he could start it swinging resulting in it bouncing off the walls and losing it's load.

The few seconds between, 'go,' and

the motor starting saw Jargodin already some five metres up the shaft.

Nick's face was pale and full of concentration as the motor strained. He had one hand on the brake lever controlling the speed and his other on the arm of the winch, making sure the wire was winding up in the centre of the shaft.

Jargodin, his adrenalin pumping, was exhilirated. He was back in the circus again. His actions were automatic.

Everyone held their breath. The only sound was that of the Honda motor and the squeal of the winch. It was frustrating not being able to actually see what was going on... Their eyes were riveted on the mouths of the shafts.

A hand grasped the galvanised pipe across the shaft, immediately followed by another: then Jargodin, catapulted out of the shaft, on to the pipe and on to solid ground... A few seconds later the bucket came into view.

The winners went wild... even some who had lost their money, could not help but acknowledge Jargodin's amazing effort. Lennie, shaking his head and laughing, made sure the winners received their money. 'I've seen every-bloody-thing,' he said.

Rosies voice once again could be heard above the crowd. 'That Jargodin, he no gammon or-right. He just like I tell him..just like 'goanna run up a tree..Aieee.'

Lennie walked over to them. He handed Jargodin and Josef their money. He was still laughing. 'Congratulations mate. Jesus,' he said, 'what next?' His tone then became serious. 'Watch your back mate. You haven't really endeared yourself to a few people today.' Jargodin nodded. He understood.

'Thanks Len.'

There was bellowing from down below. Once again Nick had forgotten about Sammy. This added to the hilarity of the occasion. It was a happy trio driving back to town. 'A good morning's work Josef?'

Josef grinned back. 'Not bad..not bad at all.'

'Oh, God, Jargodin. No more of that please. I didn't know what to think, and, to bet $500. Oh, heavens.'

Jargodin gave her a smile. 'I'll let you into a secret darling. Josef has timed me coming up a rope and many a time we have stopped by a winch and timed them. Never once have any of them been able to match my time. I've been

about five seconds faster than any we
have timed. We knew we would win and
when they had that pressure on them,
like today, that they could not lose
dirt, we knew it was in our favour.'
   'You cunning bastard,' she laughed.

CHAPTER...23.

The next two weeks passed quickly. Josef and Jargodin went out daily pillar bashing. The results were promising. They had accumulated about fifteen thousands worth of opal and were thrilled with their efforts of honest gain. Paula was happy. She had made friends with women of all nationalities. She was a good listener and would regale Jargodin with the stories of their lives as told to her. Some of the tales were amazing. Quite a few of the women, like Jargodin, had come from oveseas, fleeing from a life of poverty, and suppression.

The peace was short-lived.

Jargodin sat and listened impassively as Paula, with tears of rage, told of her ordeal. 'Look at my dress where that scum tore it.' She indicated the neck line that had been ripped down to the waist. This, to her, was the final indignation.

Jargodin had given her a nip of brandy and had calmed her down. 'Will you be okay for a while? I wont be long.'

'What are you going to do? Don't do anything silly or drastic Jargodin. He's not worth it. Forget about it.'

'Don't worry. I'm not going to do anything today. I'm going around to see Josef, but, sweetheart, there is no way I am going to let him get away with it. Nobody...but nobody, tries to molest you...understand? What I do to him will not bring any repercussions against us. There wont be any need for the law to be involved.' He laughed and leant forward and kissed her gently on her lips. He could see the concern on her face.

'I am not going to kill the bastard, he is not worth going to goal over. Don't worry honey I'll have a talk with him. Take it easy now. I'll be back soon.' Jargodin drove around to Josef's dug-out on the 'Flat,' as it was called. Lovroes car was there when he arrived. The two were seated at the table, a stubbie each, when he walked through the door.

'Oh shit, one look at that face and I see trouble,' Josef said as he got up to get a stubbie from his refrigerator.

Jargodin gave a cynical laugh. 'Hello guys. Just the two I am looking for...I could not have timed it better.'

Lovro groaned. 'Somehow I think I

should leave now.'

Josef slid a stubbie across to Jargodin now seated. 'Okay, break it gently without the frills. When do you want to rob the bank?'

Jargodin laughed. 'No, nothing like that. You know I have turned over a new leaf. No, I have a small problem.' He took a sip of his beer.

'That lay preacher, or whatever he is supposed to be, down at the church... Bellino. Un-beknown to me, for weeks now, he has been making passes at Paula. As you know, each time she goes to town, she has to drop into the church. She has been brought up on religion... you know what these Sicilians are like, especially, the Mafia women.'

'The husbands are up to their ears in crime, and the women are either in the kitchen, or in the church, lighting candles, saying the rosary or praying to the Virgin Mary. It seems to be part of the marriage contract. They have to get a credit balance of devotion so they can all pretend their wealth and their husbands actions are justified. It eases their conscience.'

'Anyhow, that is Paula's way, and I don't knock it... I guess I could do with the prayers. Paula thinks the underground church is really something and likes dropping in as often as she can. The only trouble has been that this bastard always seems to appear out of nowhere, and, she says, he is half drunk every time, and reeks of alcohol.

'This morning she went down town. On the way back from Beppe's, she dropped in to the church. As she was coming out, this prawn emerges from that room at the entrance and blocks her way. She tries to step around him, but he grabs her and tries to kiss her. She starts to struggle and he goes overboard and tries to drag her into that room.'

'Paula starts to fight like a wildcat and knees him in the crutch. He screams in pain and lets her go. She raced outside, got in the car and came home breaking every speed limit. In the tussle her dress was ripped from the neckline to the waist..She is okay now...She has settled down. I can't stay long as I don't want to leave her alone for any length of time. I am going to fix this bastard and I need your help.

'Ah, shit, I wonder what it feels like to be an accomplice to murder?' Josef said.

Lovro laughed. 'Hang around and you'll find out.'

Jargodin grinned and looked at his friends. 'No, nothing as drastic as that. I.....'

'Thank God for that,' Josef said.

'No, I just want to teach him a lesson. You don't have to be involved in the actual doing of what I have in mind. I just want you to set up a couple of things for me, if you would.'

Josef and Lovro looked at each other and laughed. 'Here we go again,' Josef said. 'Ok, paisano, what do you want us to do?'

'You know that turn off to Ice Cream hill where Johnny Bondrea lives? They both nodded. 'If you take a right turn off that track you come to that old open cut. In the side of that cut somebody cut three dug-outs.' Both men were nodding their heads. They knew the place. 'Now these dug-outs had to be abandoned as the ground was too unstable. The ceilings kept falling in. You with me?' They nodded.

'Josef have you still got that vice on that bench in your shed?'

'Yes, sure. It's still there. It's a heavy bastard.'

'Good. All the better. How big is it?'

'The bench is about five feet long. Nearly two metres: about a metre wide and not quite a metre high, but, like I said, it is heavy. The vice is bolted on to a railway sleeper.'

'Great. Can two men handle it?'

'Yeah, sure.'

'Okay. I want to buy it off you as it will be no good after I've finished with it.'

'What the bloody hell are you up to?' Josef laughed. 'You can have it. I never use it anyway.'

'Right, now this is what I want you and Lovro to do. I want you to take that vice on it's bench, out to that middle dug-out out there. It is the best one for my purpose. It has the narrowest doorway. Before you do, I want you to cut one of the knobs off the handle of the vice with your oxy torch. I want to be able to take that handle out. Capisce?' Josef nodded.

'When you have done that I want you to go to the dump and get loads of old cartons and paper and a half a dozen old tyres. I want you to half fill that joint with old rubbish that will burn, and burn well.'

'You are not going to have a cremation are you, although why you need a vice, I don't know.' Lovro said. 'What are you up to?'

'No worries. I'll tell you later, but first, can you do this for me? You will have to do it tonight, as I don't want anyone to see you.'

Josef leant back in his chair and laughed. 'Welcome to the club, Lovro. Never a dull moment. Come on Jargodin, you have to let us in on it all. What are you going to do?'

'No, I don't want you guys involved. If you can do that for me, I'll be ever grateful. Tomorrow morning I will go around and pick up our friend Bellino and take him out there and teach him a lesson.' There was silence.

'Listen mate. We come with you tomorrow morning as well, or we don't do a bloody thing. Right Lovro?'

'Right. All the way or not at all.'

Jargodin knew they meant what they said. He looked from one to the other. 'Okay, it's a deal. I'll be here at half past eight in the morning.'

Paula stood beside the car door, the depth of her concern showed on her face. 'Hurry back. I'll be worried sick. Please don't do anything foolish. Promise me Jargodin...he's not worth it. I will never forgive myself if anything happens to you.'

'Don't worry darling. Trust me. I have to do this. Nothing drastic...I'll tell you about it when I return. I'm just going to have a quiet little talk with him. No violence...Promise.'

Once again her mood change took him by surprise. Her face tightened as her eyes flashed. 'If anything happens to you, I will slit his guts open.'

'Holy Jesus,' he exclaimed. 'One minute you're saying forget him and the next minute, you're going to slit his guts open...Madonna!' They both laughed. He kissed her quickly and drove off. 'What a bloody woman,' he laughed to himself. 'Bellinoes dug-out is in that side lane beside the church. It's a dead end and there won't be a soul around. He parks his car outside his front door. I will pull in behind his vehicle. When we get there, Josef, I want you to knock and get him to open up. Speak in Italian...it will allay any suspicion. I will stand at the side from which the door swings open. As soon as it does, I will step in and take over.

'Once I have him, we tie his legs but allow about twelve centimetres between them so he can balance and won't fall when he stands. We tie his hands behind his back and tie a cloth between his teeth. When we have him trussed up we throw him in the passenger seat of his car. I will drive that. Nobody here takes the keys out of their cars, so they should be in the ignition. It they're not, they wont be hard to find. You guys then follow me in my car.

'We'll go straight out to the open cut. It will be better if I follow close behind you. It will give me some protection from being seen. From that end of the town we should be out of sight in no time. Anyhow, nobody will take any notice of us. Okay let's go.

Lovro and Josef nodded. 'Make sure you take that cap off when you are driving his car...it's a dead give-away,' Josef said.

'No worries, I will.'
Josef knocked heavily on the door. 'Bellino, Bellino. Per favore.'

A muffled reply came from within. 'Per favore Bellino.'

'Una momento. Una momento,' came the reply. They waited. The unmistakeable sound of a bolt being withdrawn, a knob being turned, then the door swung inwards.

Jargodin quickly stepped around and inside. Bellinoes mouth dropped open, his round eyes filled with fear. His pudgy face paled. He did not see the punch. He had no chance. Jargodin's right hand flashed to the side of his jaw. Bellinoes knees buckled and he started to fall. Jargodin quickly grabbed him.

'Shit, the bastard never knew what hit him,' Lovro said.

'First rule of survival,' Jargodin muttered. 'Never give a mug an even break.' He was all business. He took rope and cloth from his pockets and in no time Bellino was tied, gagged, and bundled into his own car. The keys were in the ignition.

'Come on,' Jargodin said. 'Let's get this circus on the road. I'll follow you.' It was only when they pulled up outside the room in the abandoned open-cut that Bellino stirred. Jargodin got out of the car and went into the room. A quick look around got his instant approval. The room was half choked with easy burning rubbish...the only clear space was in front of the bench, which was up against the wall near the entrance. He nodded his satisfaction and walked back to the car.

'Josef, will you and Lovro bring his Emminence in and stand him up in front of the bench. I have a few things to get out of my car.'

He returned with a jerry can half filled with kerosene, a pair of cotton gloves, a piece of thin strong twine, and a butcher's knife that had been honed to a razor's edge. He placed these on the bench.

Bellino had regained consciousness. Small pleading, whining sounds emerged through his gag. His eyes were wide and filled with terror. He was certain he was going to die. Jargodin's reputation convinced him of this.

'Hold on to him will you. One each side of him. I don't want him to fall over.'

Lovro had a sadistic grin on his face. 'Would you like me to hear your confession Bellino? You miserable slob.'

'No, I am afraid we can't spend all day listening to this bastard's confession, Lovro. Now hold him firmly. I don't want him to have a heart attack on us.' He picked up the butcher's knife from the bench. Bellino, thinking, this was it, twisted under Josef's and Lovro's grip and shook his head as strangled cries came from his mouth.

'Don't worry Bellino, I'm not going to kill you.'

The sag of relief at these words took his captors by surprise as they had to bear his weight.

'You can die here if you wish, but you will have a choice. Myself...I don't think you are fit to live and when I am finished with you, maybe you will wish you hadn't lived. Everyday, Bellino, everyday, you will see evidence of what you have done. Everyday you will remember.'

Bellino's half crazed eyes were awash with tears that rolled uncontrollably down his cheeks.

'Hold the bstard. Stand him up close to the vice.' He nodded his approval. 'The vice is the right height.'

He put the blade of the knife inside Bellino's belt and sliced outwards. His trousers flopped around his ankles. Another quick slice and his old fashioned underpants fell. Bellino, his milky white fat gut extended, stood paralysed with fear. Jargodin pulled on the gloves and picked up the twine.

Up until now, Josef and Lovro were not sure of Jargodin's intention. Now the picture started to unfold. Bellino's forehead was covered in sweat.

'Now, now, your Emminence. Don't pass out on us,' soothed Josef. 'Just think of all those women you have forced yourself on to... paticularly those poor peasant types who would be too frightened to talk.'

Jargodin spat to the side in distaste as he grabbed the head of Bellino's penis in his gloved hands.

'Lucky for you Bellino, you were never circumsised.' He pulled the loose foreskin well over the head of Bellino's penis. He had already made a noose in one end of the twine. He slipped the noose quickly over the loose flesh and pulled it tight. The jaws of the vice were already open. Jargodin pulled the loose flesh of Bellino's penis into the vice and hastily and callously tightened the jaws. Muffled screams came from Bellino.

Jargodin took the handle out of the vice and put it on the bench. 'We'll take that with us,' he said.

'Listen Bellino, and hear me good. Your life depends on what I am saying. You had better support your own weight now as the guys are going to take their hands away from you. If you collapse, you will be suspended by your prick. If you pass out, you are history.

'Josef, pour kerosene over the rubbish will you, then put the can and

this handle in our car. Now Bellino, listen carefully. You are lucky to be alive. I am going to set this rubbish alight. The flames, heat, and smoke will kill you if you stay here. I am going to leave this knife on the bench. All you have to do is slice through the flesh on the head of your prick and you will be free. You can become a Rabbi.
'Consider yourself lucky you bastard. Don't bother praying as I don't think you are worthy of divine intervention.'

Jargodin quickly sliced through the ropes on Bellino's ankles, his wrists and then the gag in his mouth. Howls of pain, fear, and pleading rented the air. Jargodin threw a match far back on the kerosene soaked rubbish. It caught alight immediately. He threw his gloves on the flames, placed the knife on the bench within easy reach and ran to his car.

'Come on, let's get out of here.' With Bellino's unhindered howls in their ears, they sped away.

'Fucking hell!' exclaimed Josef. 'What a way to go. Jesus.'

Lovro turned to Jargodin, who was concentrating as he drove fast along the track. 'Do you think he'll get out?'

Jargodin stole a glance at his

friend. 'He'll get out. What would you do? Stay there?'

They were heading towards the intersection of the main Sixteen mile road. As he reached it, Jargodin swung to the right instead of heading back to town. He drove some eight hundred metre, made a u turn, pulled over to the side and cut the motor.

Looking back across the flat countryside they could see smoke rising from the open cut they had just left. They sat and waited.

A trail of fast rising dust caught their attention...A speeding car came into view...Bellino's...Watching in silence, they saw the car reach the turn off and shoot of erratically towards town.

'Phew,' sighed Jargodin. He leant back against his seat and rubbed his eyes. Re-action set in...He took a firm hold of the steering wheel. 'That will teach the bastard.'

'Teach him!' Josef laughed. 'What do you reckon he will do now? How long before the police arrive?'

Jargodin looked at his mates and grinned. 'Don't worry. There wont be any police...I promise you that. Can you imagine him going to the police? No way.

What is he going to tell them? Don't worry amigoes. He'll be at the hospital now, scared he is going to bleed to death. I would love to be there to see his entry.' They laughed as they each tried to visualise the scene.

'What the fucking hell will he tell them?' Josef asked. This sent them into further peals of laughter.

'Okay, I'll drop you guys off in town. I had best get back. Paula will be worried.' Amid laughter and head shaking at what had happened he drove them to Ruffoes restaraunt. Josef and Lovro were still laughing as they got out of the car. 'Hey Jargodin,' Lovro said. 'Don't ring us, we'll ring you.' Half doubled up with laughter they walked away.

Paula ran out to the car as Jargodin pulled up. 'What happened Jargodin? Are you alright?'

He got out of the car smiling. 'Everything is fine sweetheart. I could do with a drink. Let's go inside and I'll tell you all about it.'

'Oh, Madonna, I don't know whether to laugh or cry. Oh, Maria,' she started to laugh.

'I need a shower darling after that.'

'Mind if I join you?' she asked

impishly.

'Be my guest.' Some five hours later, the people of the small mining town of Coober Pedy, hearing the familiar drone, looked up to the sky and saw the Flying Doctor's aeroplane overhead....'Someone has had an accident,' they said. 'I wonder who.'

CHAPTER. 24.

Life had returned to normal once more. Jargodin was hoping for news from Johnny Dondovic. He had a feeling it was time for them to move... To disappear with new identities. They had discussed time and time again as to where they should go. They both agreed that South America, perhaps, Argentina would suit them best.

'We'll keep the dug-out and let Josef look after it for us,' Jargodin said.

'On, heavens yes. I love this place. Who knows, after a few years away, we may be able to come back. Even if we don't wish to, Jargodin, it would be wise to hold it: who knows, in a few years, if we wished, we could sell for a decent price.'

He nodded his agreement. 'Sure it is an invesment.'

They both looked up. 'Josef is coming,' Jargodin said. They knew the sound of his utility.

'I don't know. All Johnny said was, that he wanted you both to ring, that it was urgent, and to reverse the charges. I thought I had best come immediately. I had just walked into Ruffoes when the phone call came.'

'Maybe it is about our passports,' Paula said.

'I hope you are right sweetheart. We had best get down to the post office and ring him.'

They had both squeezed into the public telephone box. 'Yes, Jargodin, Johnny. We just got your message. Good to hear your voice'

'Everything okay up there/'

'Yes, fine Johnny. What about you and the family?'

'Great, Jargodin, they send their best regards. Now listen carefully. I got a phone call from Paula's father. Her mother is seriously ill. Don't panic now. She is not going to die, but apparently it means a major operation and she wants to see Paula. They rang me. He said they had been ringing the flat all to no avail. You can bet your bottom dollar, they know where she is and that she is with you. They may have rung her flat, which you are still keeping, on the off chance she was in Adelaide for a few days. I don't think so. They have people down here who have been keeping a close eye on every move Paula has made.'

'Oh shit... I'll put her on, and come back to you. okay?'

'Yes, let me talk to her. I want to talk to you after talking to Paula.'

'Okay, Johnny. Here she is now.'

Paula could see by Jargodin's face that something was wrong. 'Johnny, this is Paula. What is the matter Johnny?'

'Everything is okay Paula, just don't panic. Your father rang me. Your mother is ill and it seems she has to have a major operation. She wants to see you. Your father insists you fly home immediately.'

'Oh, God, Johnny. Poor mama.... I do love her Johnny. She is my mother and it has been hard at times, growing up in a different culture entirely from one she did. It has been hard for me to accept the style of life she wants to force upon me. She has these unbending ways that were okay in the old country, but ways, which we, as Australians, just can't live by.'

'I understand Paula, I understand. If anything happens and you didn't go home, you would never forgive yourself. You realise of course, you will have to go by yourself. Jargodin can't go with you.'

'Oh, Madonna... Oh, God.... I'

'Look, Paula, put Jargodin back on.' Paula was pale faced as she numbly handed the phone back to Jargodin.

'Me again Johnny.'

'Right, now listen Jargodin. I do not wish to be cynical, but some how or other, I do not trust these bastards. Unfortunately, I have no way of checking as to Paula's mother's illness. She will have to go home and we will have to play it by ear. You will have to stay in Coober Pedy. Understand?'

'Yes, sure Johnny.' He lookd at his watch. 'Johnny there is a flight to Adelaide about one o'clock. She might be able to get on that. If she can, I will ring you. Can you meet her at the airport?'

'No problem. Don't worry paisano. We may be worrying over nothing.'

'I don't know Johnny. It is as if I have been waiting for something to happen. I'll ring you Johnny, and thanks.' They walked out on to the hot dusty street. 'I have to go, Jargodin.'

He nodded. 'I'll go over to Beppe's and see if you can get on Opal Air this-afternoon.' He strode over to the supermarket.

Paula, a conflict of emotions, stood

waiting. She realised the clash of lifestyles, between the old Sicilian ways and the open freedom of Australia, in thought and activity had caused differences between her and her mother. The tie of mother and daughter, however, was strong and took precedent over all else.

Deep in thought she wasn't aware of Jargodin's approach until he took her arm. She gave a start.

'You okay?'

She nodded.

'Come on, let's go home. I got you a seat on the 'Plane. We have an hour before take off.' Jargodin drove to the airport. Willy-willies spiralled to the horizon. They darted and danced across the horizon, as if in a wild, ancient, macabre ritual.

The silence hung like gloom over both of them. 'Jargodin, I don't want to leave you.'

He took his left hand off the wheel and picked up her right one and raised it to his lips. 'Don't worry, sweetheart. Everything is going to be okay.'

'I don't know. I have this feeling. I am worried.'

'It is only natural Paula. Your

mother is sick. You must go to her.
Everything will be okay. Believe me. You
must be strong.' They arrived at the
small tin shed at the airport. People
were already walking over to the small
aeroplane. They had cut it fine.

Paula only carried a small airline
bag as she had plenty of clothes in her
flat in Adelaide. It was time to part.

Paula began to cry. 'I don't want to
go.'

'You have to darling.' He took a
handkerchief from his pocket. 'Here.'

She wiped her eyes and smiled
through her tears. 'Don't you go taking
out any women while I am away, you
bastard,' she said in mock severity.
They both laughed.

'That's better,' he said. 'That is
my girl. I love that fighting spirit.
You have to go darling. I love you. You
are my whole life.'

She threw her arms around his neck.
They kissed tenderly.
'I'll ring Ruffoes darling, as soon as I
can.' She hurried across the tarmac.
Jargodin stood for a long time after the
'plane was out of sight. He just stood
looking at the horizon where it had
disappeared. He felt so alone...

CHAPTER. 25.

Two weeks had gone by. Johnny Dondovic and Josef sat at a table in Ruffoes. Johnny had flown up by Opal Air. 'I'll stay at the motel opposite Mobil tonight and fly back tomorrow. How is Jargodin?'

Josef shrugged. 'I'm not sure...He's holding himself in control. For the first week, he came down here twice a day to see if there were any messages. He hasn't been down for a week now. He comes to town, gets some beer and food and goes home. I go around every day. I suggest we go out to the field, but he just shakes his head. She is not coming back, is she?'

'No...No, unless....Let's go around and see Jargodin. I'll get some beer to take with us.'

The three men sat at the table in Jargodin's dug-out. Johnnies eyes surveyed the room. The place was clean and tidy...A good sign...A few empty stubbies were on the table when they entered. Jargodin looked well enough.

Jargodin looked squarely at Johnny. 'Okay, my friend, give it to me. You didn't come all the way from Adelaide just to say, hello.'

'She is not coming back.' Johnny sighed. 'well that is her father's view. Remember I told you over the phone, it may have been a sham?' He waited for his friends nod. 'Well, it was.' He struck the table with his open palm. 'It was a ploy to get her home. These bastards have no morals and to use such a low bloody trick, is unforgivable... We must, however, remember who we are dealing with... The bloody Mafia... The end justifies the means.

'They have no intention of letting her out of their grasp this time. Let's look at the facts as we have them. Paula's father is a capo, and a Don like him, commands a lot of respect and power. Any weakening on his part is a serious mistake. Don't for one moment think that there is no Mafia in Australia... that it is only in America and Italy. If you think that, you believe in the tooth fairy.

'Paula broke tradition once and got away with it, but a new situation has arisen. There is this guy, one of them naturally... he must be well up in the organisation... who wants to marry Paula. He has seen her and knows the family through dealings with Paula's father. He was married, but his wife died. He lives in Sydney and a marriage would be a merging of considerable interests.

'Paula's father has to show his strength and control here. He can't afford any weakness at all. You must remember, Paula's father grew up with a strict code of honour in the organisation. Marriages with another family for purely economic gain and strength, was the norm rather than a rare happening. He still believes in the code. He scorns our way here in Australia.

'You,' Johnny nodded at Jargodin, 'are not quite his idea of a son-in-law. I guess, he is not quite your idea of a father-in-law either.'

Jargodin sat grim-faced and silent. Josef listened.

'We know, they can't keep Paula under lock and key. They realise she could always get a letter to you, or somehow get you on the phone. They have told her in no uncertain terms what will happen to you if she tries. You will meet a very unpleasant end. She knows this is no idle threat. She has no choice. If, she tries to get in touch with you in any shape or form, you die, and...you die slowly and painfully.

'She loves you. She doesn't want you hurt. She wants you to live. She has no choice but to marry this other creep. So there you have it my friend.' Johnny threw his hands in the air in resignation. 'The bastards!'

Johnny got up and walked around, then came back and leant on the table. 'You travel thousands of kilometres to get away from those bastards over there and make a new life...What do you get? You find the bludgers are here! They bring their shit with them! Don't for one moment think it is only the Mafia.

'Go down to Ruffoes restaurant now...have a look around. In one corner you have a table of Serbians...in another corner, a table of Macedonians...in another, a table of Croatians, then a table of Greeks...They all hate each other's guts! Why?...Because they brought that hatred with them. They carry this poison with them. Ah, Shit,' he said in disgust.

Johnny looked at each of them. 'You two are no better. You hate the Greeks, the Serbs and the Macedonians, so it is okay to steal from them. What a bloody mess. The sins of our fathers...' his words trailed off.

'Now get this straight...both of you...I don't condole what you are doing...I have become involved because of Paula...If it wasn't for her, I would let both of you go to hell. I like you guys...I like both of you, but, you have got to promise me that there is no more...No more moonlighting.' He looked from one to the other.

'I had already promised Paula, Johnny. I have given my word.'

'Well, that is a relief. You have my full support. What about you Josef?'

'No problems, Johnny. It was adventure to me. I don't need the money. I can make it underground.'

'Good. That is settled.' Johnny sat down and locked his eyes with Jargodin's. 'Listen to me paisano. Remember, the best steel comes out of the hottest furnaces. You're young, so is Paula. Don't give up hope. Don't let this throw you. These volturnoes, these vultures, are only human, but...they are deadly. They have a network that stretches all over the world. They can,' he stressed, 'they can be beaten. The risk is great, you know that, but, look at the alternative.

'You knew the risk when you came up here. Paula knew. She was prepared to take the gamble. Now, just because the pennies have come up tails, your'e not going to throw the kip away, are you? Unless I am sadly mistaken, I believe both of you are fighters. What do you want to do?'

Jargodin looked at the penetrating eyes of his friend. He laughed and stood up. 'We fight Johnny...We will beat them.'

Johnny smiled. That is more like it. 'Let's have a drink. Have you anything to eat in this bloody place? I don't fancy eating Nick's slops.'

'Yes, the 'fridge is full of steaks.'

'Great,' Josef said. 'I'm the cook. thank God we have that all settled.' They laughed.

'You are a good cook, Josef,' Johnny said as they ate. They were hungry. The positive mood had lifted their appetites.

'It slipped my mind, but how come you have all this information. Has Paula's father told you all this.'

Johnny nodded. 'Yes. He laid the facts out without any frills. Paula has rung me also. They realise they can't keep her a prisoner and with the threat on your life, she won't do anything silly. He also told me to sell Paula's car and to give her clothes and things to some charity.

'I told him I would buy the car for Junata and see to her gear. We won't do anything yet awhile. I'll get in touch with Paula. Leave everything to me. You just stay put and don't do anything silly. Oh, by the way, the good news. I have both your passports... New identities... They may have arrived just in time.'

'Great Johnny. What about money?'

'No, I still have plenty of yours left. I called in a few outstanding favours. Incidentally, you have developed quite a reputation down south. Seems everone has heard about your skill at coming up a rope.'

Josef laughed. 'Ah, Jesus, Johnny. you should have been there.' He went on to tell the tale. They tidied the dugout and went down town to have a few drinks at Ruffoes. New life had come into Jargodin's step. He knew, somewhere along the line, something had to happen... it had... now it had to be met...

CHAPTER. 26.

Jargodin busied himself around the dug-out for a few days. Each day he lived in hope of word from Johnny. None came. He spent more time down at Ruffoes with Josef and other miners. The days dragged on and still no word. He was now drinking on a regular basis and drinking alone back at the dug-out. Josef was worried.

Ten days had passed when Johnny rang Ruffoes. Jargodin was there at the time with Josef. He answered the phone...Josef saw the grim look on Jargodin's face as he returned to the table. He waited for his friend to speak.

'She is not coming back. The risks are too great. She rang Johnny. They have really scared the living daylights out of her. Her father has told her that unless she comes to her senses now, they are going to take me out immediately. She told Johnny to tell me to leave the country and make a new life for myself. She will just have to do what they want. As a matter of fact she has agreed to everything they say.'

'Oh, Jesus, amigo. I don't know what to say.'

Jargodin gave Josef a wry grin. 'Don't worry mate.... I think I'll get a carton and go home.'

'Do you want me to come around?'

'No...No...I've got to work this out.' Jargodin stayed on a bender for a week. He was seen in town occasionally. His stay would be brief. He was quiet and withdrawn. A few drinks at the hotel...buy some cartons, then back to his dug-out was the routine...At home he drank himself into oblivion.

Josef was surprised. It was mid-afternoon. He walked into Jargodin's dug-out and looked around. The place was spotless.

Jargodin saw the look of amazement on Josef's face. 'Yeah. I decided it was time to call a halt. I took all the empty stubbies down to the dump. The joint smelt of stale beer and cigarette smoke. It, as well as myself needed a bloody good cleaning. Feel like a beer?'

Josef nodded. 'Good. I'll join you. It's my first for the day and I need it. I have been putting it off, hour by hour. I need a few to settle my bloody nerves.' He got two stubbies out of the refrigerator.

'Ah, God, that's good,' he said as he drank a few sips. 'I hung one on but...' Arm extended, he held his hand straight out. 'No shakes,' he muttered.

'You look okay. You've come out of it well. Boy, you sure had me worried. Knowing you, I didn't know what to expect. I thought you might go up there to Ingham and blast the whole family.'

'The thought entered my mind,' Jargodin laughed.

'What are you going to do?'

'I'm doing one more job then I'll leave.'

'You promised Johnny...'

'No, I promised Paula. There is a difference. Anyhow, it doesn't matter now.'

'Jargodin, give it away. You have enough money. Piss off somewhere. Go overseas as Paula suggests.'

Jargodin's jaw tightened. His eyes half closed. 'I'm not going overseas for those bastards. I left overseas to get away and start a new life. They have Paula, but they aren't running me out of this country. I like it too much. Somewhere along the line... Somewhere, I'll get my own back. Not now, not for a long time... I'll let them think they have won. After a while they will forget all about me. That is when I'll hit. I'll never forget.'

Josef shrugged. 'Why do another job? Give it away now.'

'No. Tom Tom came around just before you arrived. Charlie sent him around with a message. Pasquallie is on opal...It's an open cut. Seems they had just started to rip this-morning and they struck opal. They had only ripped a metre and they turned it up.

'Apparently they have been digging it out all day and have only gone a little over two metres. It must be a big pocket. Pasquallie owes me. He tried to clip me in a card game one night. This is my last job. This one and I am away.

'I need the help of two more guys. Do you know a couple who could be interested?'

'Shit, I can get you a dozen. Two...Yes, no problem...Milan and Tony. You can trust them with your life...They wont talk...Wait a minute...Pasquallie...He has that mad Czechoslavakian out there as night watchman. That crazy bastard with a beard...Machine gun Joe they call him. He had a big write up in the Geographical magazine recently. Forget it amigo. Leave it be.'

Jargodin laughed. 'No worries. It will be a piece of cake. Anyhow, you tell these guys about Machine Gun Joe and if they don't want to be in it, no problem. I was going to do it on my own, but with another two to help, it will make it all the quicker.'

'Ah, hell, you're bloody crazy. Count me in.'

'No way...You promised Johnny remember. You keep your slate clean.'

'Listen. I couldn't care less about the opal. You promise me this is the last.' Jargodin nodded. 'Good. I'm coming to see you don't do anything stupid. Johnny would never forgive me if I let you out of my sight. Oh, Madre Mio. I used to know a time when things were nice and peaceful.'

Jargodin laughed. He had come alive once more. 'I'll meet you and the other two a few hundred metres along the turn off to the Eleven Mile field. That is where he is operating. We'll meet about eight o'clock. Okay?'

'Okay paisano. My retirement was shortlived, but, last one huh?'

'I promise.' Jargodin threaded his way along the well worn track. Driving with no lights, the track still stood out in relief with the aid of a half moon. Josef and his friends were pulled off to the side waiting. As he passed he waved them to follow. Slowly he wound his way deeper into the field. He pulled up beside a large open cut. It was about seventy metres long, forty metres wide, and thirteen metres deep. In the dim light below, the outline of a bulldozer could be seen.

The four men stood looking down. Jargodin knew the men who had come with Josef. He trusted Josef's judgement.

'Where do we go?' Milan asked. Jargodin pointed to the cut below.

'Don't tell me we have to dig it up with picks?'

'No way. I'm going to drive the bulldozer.'

'What?' a stunned Tony asked. 'Are you crazy?'

'No problem. They're on opal. We start the 'dozer up, do a few short rips...the 'dozer has lights, front and back..we get what we want and get out of the joint.'

'Holy shit! I've heard everything!' Milan said. He thought for a few seconds and then quietly laughed. 'Of all the bloody cheek.'

Josef nudged Jargodin's arm. He

pointed to the caravan at the far end of the cut. A light was on inside. 'What about his nibs in there?' He must have heard our approach.'

'He has heard us for sure. A still night like this, noise carries for miles. He is in there wondering what the hell is going on. Don't worry. He's no hero. He's only sixty cents in the dollar, poor bastard. He'll be no problem. Wait here.'

Jargodin walked to his car and came back cradling his. He had dug it up from where it had been buried all this time. He had cleaned off all the grease. He inserted a clip.

'Jesus...What are you going to do? Listen mate, I don't feel like being involved in murder. That is too much for me. Count me out,' Tony said.

'Yeah, me too,' said Milan. Josef was even taken back at the sight of the machine gun.

Jargodin laughed quietly. 'Don't worry. I'm not going to kill the poor bastard. I'm not that bloody silly. Wait here. I wont be long.'

Jargodin cautiously walked over to the caravan. He approached it from the rear. He stopped about thirty yards away, well outside the light that shone through the windows.

His eyes had adjusted to the dim countryside. He looked all around. Everything was quiet and still. He imagined that Joe was in there in one hell of a panic, wondering what the hell was going on...He would be scared...Of that there was no doubt, but as Jargodin knew, a scared person could do strange things.

'Hello, Joe. Can you hear me? Joe, can you hear me?'

'Whose there? What you want? You shouldn't be here. I have a gun.'

'Yes, sure, Joe. I know you have a gun. Now why don't you come outside without your gun and we will talk.'

'You had better go, or I will shoot.'

Jargodin lifted the Schmisser, aimed high, and sent a stream of bullets across the caravan tearing holes just under the roof.

Josef, Milan and Tony were taken by surprise. 'Jesus,' gasped Milan.

'Stay down low Joe.' He unleashed another burst in the same area.

'No more! No more!' Joe screamed. 'Stop! Stop! Don't kill me. Don't kill me. What do you want?'

'Just come out and around Joe and

stand in the light. We wont hurt you. I promise. Come out with your hands clear. We wont hurt you.'

'How do I know I can trust you. Who are you?' Joe was frantic.

'It's Jargodin Joe. Come on. I don't wont to hurt you.'

'Oh, shit Jargodin. You know me. What do you want to do this to me for?'

'Okay Joe. Now, if you don't come out now, I am going to put two more full clips into the van. This time the shots will be lower. You had better come out Joe.'

'I'm coming. I'm coming.' Joe shot out of the caravan and around to the end. Arms high above his head, he stood trembling in the light cast from the window. He was petrified.

Jargodin smiled at Joe as he walked towards him. 'Don't worry Joe. No-one is going to hurt you. You just do what I say and everything will be okay. We have some business down in the cut. It wont take long. Now what I am going to do, is to tie you up. That way, when they come out in the morning, you will be okay. You can tell them, some guys in masks pulled a gun on you. You had no chance. Understand?'

'Yes, sure, Jargodin. Joe's

composure was returning. He wasn't going to be killed... There was hope.

'But, of course, Joe, you don't know who they were. they were all masked.'

'Don't worry, Jargodin. Don't worry,' Joe blustered. 'I didn't see anyones face.'

'Good, Joe. Just as long as we understand each other.'

'No worries. Jargodin. No worries.'

Joe was tied ... The bull-dozer was started. The ground was ripped revealing opal of top red quality. Four, twenty litre buckets were filled.

Before leaving, Jargodin told Joe in no uncertain terms, what would happen to him if he talked. 'Don't forget Joe, there are three guys with me who you didn't see. If anything happens to me, they will fix you for good. They are bad bastards.'

Joe vowed complete ignorance.

The next day, the robbery was the talk of the town. Of all the cheek... to drive the bulldozer and rip at night... Where will it all end?

A very drunk, Joe was seen hanging on to the bar mumbling, 'I know nothing... I know nothing.' His career as a nightwatchman was short lived, but there were compensations... He found a large envelope on the table in his dug-out, containing $5,000. The words, SILENCE IS GOLDEN, were printed on the envelpoe together with the instructions, 'please burn.'

Joe was happy. Being a nightwatchman was not so bad after all.
Jargodin returned to his dug-out. There was no feeling of exhiliration. He felt lost and lonely...there was a sense of betrayal. he sat at the kitchen table drinking stubbies. Paula...he could see her, talking, laughing, making love...Alcohol eventually took over...He staggered to bed and slept. In North Queensland his fate was being formed.

CHAPTER. 27.

'Who can that be, I wonder?' June got up to answer the phone. It was ten o'clock at night. She and Johnny were sitting at the kitchen table drinking coffee. The conversation was about Paula and Jargodin.

'Johnny,' she hurried back to the kitchen. 'Bruno on the line for you. Paula's brother,' she spoke urgently. Johnny ran to the phone in the lounge.

Jesus, what now? he thought. 'Yes, Johnny here Bruno.'

'Johnny, listen carefully. Paula and I have had a long talk. I will do anything I can to help her out of this mess. She says, she would rather be dead than married to this bloody Mafioso. Now, I don't want my sister dead, or married to this bastard. Can you hear me?'

'Yes, sure, I hear you loud and clear.'

'Well, I don't believe in all this shit. I am an Australian...period..I play football up here, I'm in the lifesavers, and I just want a normal life. I want nothing to do with this Black Hand business. Do you understand?'

'Yeah, I understand perfectly.'

'The trouble is, Father is tied up with them and tied up deep. It goes way back and apparently, he owes a couple of favours...big ones...from the old country...I don't know what they are, and I don't want to know. Anyhow these favours are now being called in...Paula is part of the deal. Capisce?

'Yes, sure, carry on.'

'Back in Sicily, living the old way, Paula would have done what he wanted. It was an accepted thing. It would be no big deal...The problem is, some of them can't get it through their heads, that it is not acceptable to us growing up in this country.

'Unless father sticks to what is expected of him, he is finished. He would be 'maladetta.' It all depends on who is calling in the chips. It has to be someone at the top...someone who believes the code must be honoured to the full. He could pay the supreme price by the traditional shotgun.

'Now, if Paula somehow manages to flee...to disappear entirely on her own, that would be a different scenario..Sure, dad would cop a lot of flack...lose respect and no doubt hit him hard money wise. He would be out, but he could at least be allowed to live.'

'We have plenty of money... We don't need all this other bullshit, but it is more than that... it's power. Power is the name of the game. Power and the fear it has with it..'

'Let's say, Paula shoots through. There will be a big hunt for her... Let's not kid ourselves. They have known ever move she has made, since leaving home.

'The biggest problem we would have, is this hit man she is to marry... Lou Corotto. I know him... he has been up here. I first met him in Sydney. His first wife died. He is one of those smooth, good looking, Latin types... real Hollywood gangster types... He tries to act that way. He loves himself... He has, I believe, put away a few, as the saying goes.'

'Well this guy would be humiliated, so much so, that he would immediately be out for revenge. He is an egotistical bastard who would have to do it himself... on his own. He would have no hesitation of going up there to Coober Pedy and blasting Jargodin. What he would do to Paula, I do not know
The part that worries me Johnny, is, that no matter where Paula and Jargodin

run to, they would eventually be found. I have talked this over with Paula. I have told her, that somewhere, someday, they will find her. She understands, but says that providing Jargodin is willing to take the risk, she is ready...Jesus, what has this guy got. I haven't met him, but, shit, I....'

'Yeah, well Bruno, he is one rare character, believe me. To be honest, I have never seen two people more suited...It's unbelievable. Listen, my brain has been ticking over while you have been talking...Incidentally, where are you ringing from?'

'It's okay. I'm ringing from a mate's place in town. Never mind the cost, that's nothing.'

'Good. I think we have been looking at this all wrong. We can beat these bastards. The important thing is whether you can keep me informed of what is going on.'

'What I can do is this, providing Paula can get away. I...'

'Can you get Paula to the aerodrome in Ingham by about eight in a morning?'

'Ye...es. Yes, sure.'

'Right. Providing you can get her there around that time, I will have a small private aeroplane waiting. The plane will cut across inland Queensland...over Lake Eyre and on to Coober Pedy. It will take nearly all day as they will have to refuel...Those things can be arranged. If you can get her in to catch that 'plane, we will do the rest.'

'Yes, I can do that.'

'Good. Now is there any way you can let me know what is happening at your end?'

'The best I can do is this. All telephone calls from the farm, go through a small local exchange up at Stone River. I know the people who run the exchange; as a matter of fact I play football with the son. He is a close friend of mine. He speaks Italian and can understand Sicilian.'

'I will make sure he mans the exchange for as long as necessary. He is always ringing me and passing on messages and I spend a lot of time with him. He will let me know the full gist of every message sent from the farm. I will then let you know.'

'That is all I want. Now listen carefully Bruno. I will have a small 'plane standing by at the Ingham aerodrome ready to take off at eight o'clock in the morning, the day after tomorrow. It is Tuesday night now, so you have her there Thursday morning. Can you do that?'

'Yes, I can. She will be there. Jesus, Maria, as a kid growing up, I never dreamed that these sort of things could happen in this country.'

'I know what you mean. Have you ever thought to yourself, how many other Paulas and Brunoes, are going through, or have gone through a similar situation...All this bloody bullshit we don't want in this country. Thank God there are people like yourself and Paula who are prepared to break the chain. I had to do it myself at the risk of my family.'

'Yeah, that is all bloody fine, but Paula's life is on the line here.'

'Yes, I understand. So is Jargodin's. Leave it with me. I am confident we can win this. I am not going to tell you what I have in mind...Rest assured, everything will be okay.'

'I pray to God, you are right.'

'Incidentally, what does this Lou guy look like?'

'On the old scale about five foot nine...I don't know what that is in centimetres. Well built...dark waving hair...He's a good looking bastard, but he carries that arrogant smirk..He's about thirteen stone.'

'Good. Don't worry. Now get ready to take down this phone number. I am flying to Coober Pedy tomorrow. This number will get me or a message to me in a matter of minutes. You have my home number so you can keep in touch with June if necessary.'

Johnny passed on the phone number. The conversation was ended. He walked back into the kitchen.

'Oh, oh. I can tell by the look on your face, something is brewing.'

Johnny laughed. 'You know me too well. Yes...We are going to beat these bastards.'

June's eyes shone. 'I'm so glad . Poor Paula...I could cry when I think of what she is going through.'

'I have a lot to do...I had best make some calls..now.'

CHAPTER. 28.

Jargodin heard Josef's utility pull up outside the dug-out. He was sitting at the table, a stubbie in his hand, six empties in front of him. He was not prepared for Josef's excited entry.

'Jargodin, Jargodin,' eyes alight, Josef burst into the room. 'Paula will be here on Thursday. Johnny arrives tomorrow. They...'

Jargodin had come alive. 'Hold it, hold it, steady...What the hell are you saying?' He looked at his friend in disbelief.

'Give me a fucking chance and I'll tell you,' Josef laughed.

Paula, Jargodin, Josef and Johnny sat around the table in Jargodin's dug-out. Paula had arrived at the Coober Pedy airport just before dark. Jargodin had been waiting a good two hours before her arrival. His thoughts full of, 'what ifs,' he had scanned the skies consistently. Eventually it all happened. The small 'plane touched down and Paula was soon in his arms crying with relief and happiness.

Johnny had discreetly given them time alone before he and Josef had arrived with barbecue chickens and cold drinks. The reunions were heart warming and sincere. They had eaten and now sat seriously contemplating the problems at hand. Jargodin sat beside Paula his comforting arm around her shoulder.

'You just cannot keep running. You can't run from these people forever...their tentacles spread all over the world. We have to make a stand, confuse them, falsify things and disappear. These people are old hands at this sort of thing. Paula's father is a big wheel in this organisation. I made it my business to find out.

'He has been embarassed once by Paula...He managed to smooth that over...This time he can't afford any mistakes. As it is, this will cause a lot of waves. You have to be eliminated Jargodin.' Paula paled as Johnnies words forced the reality upon them.

'You can be sure, someone is already on their way or making plans. My bet, is that it will be Corotto. He will have to do this himself. He is a known hit man. His honour is at stake. His ego demands satisfaction.

'I am convinced there is at least

one of the mob living here in Coober Pedy. There has to be. They have known too much. They have known every bloody move. Probably someone who has done good service and has been allowed to do his own thing here, but they are never retired. They are always available if called upon.

'Both of you have to be ready to leave at a moment's notice. Just a small travelling case each with a few personal things. Everything else is to be left here. Josef will look after it all.

'You have to trust me entirely,' he stressed as he looked from one to the other....

'No problem Johnny. We are in your hands...Whatever you say, we do.'

'Good that is the way it has to be. I have already got things rolling. I must say this once more. You must do things exactly as I say. It is vital...I'll tell you more tomorrow.'

Johnny seemed to command confidence. His arranging of the aeroplane at such short notice already earned their respect. How like my father he is in many respects, thought Paula. The big difference is that he is his own man and not one of some secret organisation that rules through fear.

'Josef and I will leave you two. I am sure you have a lot to talk about.' He gave a wry grin. 'Tonight you are safe. Tomorrow...a different ball game. Remember, he only wants you Jargodin.'

'Yes that is a comforting thought,' Jargodin said. They smiled at his cynical reply.

'I'll be back in the morning. I've a room at the back in Ruffoes. Use the back entrance if you need me. Ciao. Sleep tight.' Clear blue skies heralded another day on the opal field. As the day progressed, the wind would strengthen; willy willies would dance and spiral their dusty chimneys to the heavens as they wove back and forth in a wild macombo across the plains. Miners were already making their way out to the fields. To most, another normal day.

An early model Holden was parked just off the airport boundary. A jack under the axle lifted the back passenger side whel off the ground. Nearby lay a spare wheel. Two male aboriginees sat in the shade of the car. They sat silent, crossed legged and impassive. An aboriginal woman and two piccaninnies squatted among the short stunted growth. With her digging stick she probed in the sandy soil under the bush for grubs and small lizards. She was within hailing distance of the men.

At the Golden Fleece service station, at the entrance to town, Charlie and Gunya, another aboriginee, sat on the cement wall near the road. They blended in with the nearby activity and didn't receive more than a passing glance. They sat and waited.

When the Mobil restaurant opened above the service station, Tony and Milan, entered and took seats by the window. From here they had a clear view of the motel opposite.

An aeroplane came in low over the horizon, circled and landed. As it did, a car trailing a cloud of dust, drove up to the small shed that acted as the terminal. A man alighted from the 'plane and quickly made his way to the waiting vehicle. As soon as the man entered the car, it turned and headed back to town.

One of the aboriginal men walked over to the woman and children. He bent down. Immediately a wisp of smoke drifted skywards.

Charlie and Gunya spotted the smoke almost simultaneously. They signalled to another aboriginee man sitting in a vehicle across the street. All traffic from the airport had to pass their way.

Charlie got up and walked behind Ruffoes. He knocked on a door of a room.

A dust covered Holden pulled up at the motel opposite Mobil. The passenger, dressed in a sombre suit, alighted. With a small travelling bag in hand, he made his way to the reception. Another badly dented Holden pulled up on the vacant strip some fifty metres away. An aborigine got out and lifted the bonnet. He peered into the motor for a few seconds then closed the bonnet. He gave the hood a couple of satisfied taps, climbed back in then drove away.

'That's our baby,' Milan whispered excitedly to Tony. Tony nodded.

The man came out of reception and made his way around the side of the building. He indicated his direction to the driver of his vehicle. The car backed up, swung in the direction shown and pulled up before the door. The passenger inserted the key, opened the door and went inside. The driver got out of the car and followed.

'I know that bastard,' Tony breathed.

'Yes, so do I,' Milan said. 'He's the one who sliced up that young Australian lad in the pub a couple of years ago. Nothing came of it.

Sergio...that's the bastard. I had better ring Johnny.' Milan got up. A few words to the barman and he went into the office to make his call.

The two men emerged from the motel. Sergio stood by his car door and pointed across the road to to Mobil. The other man nodded and began to walk over.

'Come on,' Milan said. 'It's lunch time. He's coming for a meal. Let's follow Sergio.' As they reached the bottom of the stairs, the stranger was only a few metres away and approaching. They walked casually to their car.

'Mmm. Smart looking character,' Tony said. 'Looks a bit out of place out here.'

'I guess he is not here for a holiday,' Milan replied. 'Come on. We've got to get behind Sergio. I know where he lives so does Josef. They should be there waiting. He lives around by Fleming's butcher shop. We are assuming he is going home.' Sergio's car was out of sight. 'Put your foot down and head around the back way. Go straight to his dug-out. Josef and Jargodin would be there now waiting. They would have gone there as soon as I rang Johnny.' Tony nodded.

As Sergio got out of his car, Josef

and Jargodin, who were parked over the road and back a bit, ran towards him. Tony and Milan just pulled up. They immediately got out and headed to Sergio. Sergio heard Josef and Jargodin's approach and swung around. A look of alarm crossed his face. Tony and Milan were now upon him from behind. Sergio panicked, but all too late. He had no chance. He was quickly tied and bundled into Jargodin's station wagon. Both cars hurriedly left the scene.

Jargodin headed out on the dusty road past the Jungle, so called for the half dozen trees that grew there. Tony and Milan followed at a distance that allowed the dust of Jargodin's vehicle to clear by the cross wind. Too close made visibility practically nil.

It was a deserted area. Jargodin swung off the main thoroughfare on to one of the many tracks that disappeared behind some old dumps. He pulled up well clear of the road. Tony and Milan were soon there. Sergio lay spreadeagled on the ground tied to stakes driven well into the hard surface. Hate blazed out of his dark eyes. He gritted his teeth as he muttered curses.

'All I want to know, is what arrangements you have made with our friend at the motel' Sergio spat at Jargodin, the spittle falling harmlessly to the side.

'I wouldn't waste your spit Sergio. It is already hot and getting hotter. Not a very sensible thing to do.' Jargodin walked back to the cars where his friends stood watching and waiting. He took out a litre container of honey. He walked back to his victim.

Jargodin ripped Sergio's shirt open and poured honey over his chest and down into his waist. He undid his trousers and poured honey down his crutch. He emptied the container and tossed it aside.

He squatted down beside Sergio and watched. His expression was devoid of any mercy. 'You will talk Sergio. You will talk.' He got up and walked back to his mates.

They sat in Jargodin's car, watched and waited. No-one spoke. They each lived this scene in their own way. The ants were swarming over Sergio. His muttered curse now became cries and stifled screams.

Sergio twisted his body back and forth as much as his bonds would allow. His screams became louder. He cursed. He sobbed. The ants took no notice.

'Jesus, I don't know how much more I can take, let alone that poor bastard,' Tony said.

Jargodin nodded. 'I understand, but don't forget that poor bastard was going to help put me away, and, for good. It won't be long now. Too much of this and he could end up a raving lunatic. I don't want that to happen. The sun beating straight down can do enough damage without the ants.'

'Jeez, what a way to go,' Milan said.

'I'll try him out now. I think he has had enough.' Jargodin walked back. 'You ready to talk Sergio?' Sergio nodded his head vigourously. He was covered in ants. The torment was horrific.

'Josef will you bring me that twenty litre drum of water from the back of the car please.'

Jargodin poured the water over Sergio's body. The relief was immediate. 'Right, now talk. I promise you your life if you tell the truth. If you tell me lies, you are dead. Tell me what I want to know. We will then take you out to a field. You will be let down a shaft with food and water and a torch.'

'I know this shaft well. There is a

small drive in it, so you will have plenty of room to move about. Providing you are telling the truth, someone will be there in two days time with a set of ladders to let you out. If what you tell me is wrong, someone will be there with a bull-dozer to fill the shaft in. You have my word. I promise this on my mother's life.'... The ultimate oath.

Sergio was sobbing and on the verge of hysteria. Jargodin's words penetrated through his torment. He had no choice...Cristo, a gun, a knife, he could understand, but this... this was...He couldn't describe it...He knew Jargodin would keep his word. He had sworn the oath. Shit, let me out of here...To be buried alive if he didn't tell the truth had it's horrors...No more. Madre Mio...No more. The words gushed out of his mouth.

CHAPTER. 29

Jargodin slumped over the table knocking a half full stubbie of beer over in the process. 'Hell,' Josef said and walked over to the bar. 'Give me a cloth Patrick will you. I want to clean up this mess.'

Patrick, the barman, handed him a dish-rag. 'what the bloody hell has happened to Jargodin? I have never seen him drunk like this.'

'Ah, he has been drinking all day. Paula came back last night to pick up her things... she is leaving him. He reckons he is going to blow his brains out. He says, he can't live without her. I don't know what to do? I'll take him home to my place.'

'Yes. Good idea. Jesus, you had better keep him locked up. He's capable of anything. If he said he will blow his brains out, bet your life he will.'

'I know. I'll have to do something. I'll take him home. Paula is scared out of her wits.'

'She has got good bloody reason to be, if you ask me.'

The rumour spread. Jargodin was drunk and was going to kill himself.

The last red glow on the horizon had faded as night took over. A half intoxicated, tall thin aborigine knocked on the door of the motel room.

'Sergio?' questioned a voice from inside. The knock came again.

'I got message for mister in this room.' He staggered as he spoke.

The curtain of the window parted and a face peered out. All he could see was an aborigine swaying slightly in front of his door. He rapped sharply on the glass. The aborigine gave a bit of a start and looked at the face in the window. His mouth opened in a wide grin. He walked to the window.

'One man, he tell me come here and say to you, his car come bugger-up, finish. He try to fix 'im. If he can't fix 'im, he say, you go over road, have some tucker. Him fella get 'nother car and come bye 'n bye soon.'

A triumphant grin spread over the aborigine's face. He had done what he was told. He started to stagger off. The man in the room heard the message, but was uncertain. He quickly opened the door and called out to the retreating back of the messenger.

'Hey, what you say?'

The aboriginee turned back to the

man. 'I bin tell you. One man, his car come bugger-up, finish. He say, tell man this room,' he pointed to the door. 'Tell man, go eat tucker. He come soon.'

'Where you see this man?'

'Aahh...That way.' He pointed in the direction of The Flat. 'This fella live not far from me fella. I know long time. I bin come town. This fella stop me, ask come tell you. He no fix car, he get 'nother one.' He gave a wide grin. 'He bin give me five dollar. I bin tell you. I go.' He staggered off into the night. When he was well out of sight, he straightened up and chuckled to himself.

The man swore under his breath and went back to his room. 'I'd best eat,' he muttered.

CHAPTER. 30.

A young police constable walked into the Police station. The sergeant looked up. 'How's the town Bill? Quiet?'

'Yeah, seems so...except this Jargodin fella.' He shook his head in deep thought.

'What about him?'

'Apparently, he is as drunk as a monkey getting about town. Word has it, that his shiela has come back only to pack up and leave. He has been raving on about how he is going to kill himself if she does...I don't know...doesn't sound like the Jargodin we know.'

The Sergeant thought awhile...'Yes, I see what you mean.' He shrugged. 'You never know with these guys Bill...You know, some of them carry a heavy load from their past overseas. It only needs some little thing to trigger them off. That combined with a gut full of booze....' His voice trailed off.

'Look Bill, drive aroud to their dug-out and check up on the woman. See how she is...If he kills himself, that's okay. I won't cry, but check on her.'

'Sure, Serge.' Paula heard the noise of a strange vehicle. It was a police van. 'Oh, God,' she muttered to herself. 'The tobacco. I hope you're right Johnny.' She took a pinch of tobacco out of a packet lyng on a bench. She put a bit in each eye and rubbed vigourously. 'Mumma Mia,' she gasped. It stung like hell.

The policeman came to the door just as Paula had rinsed her face unde the tap. Her reddened eyes told him the story of her grief.

'Just checking ma'am. I heard you may have had a bit of trouble. Are you alright?'

Paula gave an embarrased subdued smile as she wiped her eyes. 'Yes, officer. Thank you for coming. I'm okay. I was a bit scared, but I am going down the road to stay with some friends of mine for the night. I shall be leaving tomorrow.'

The policeman hesitated...She is a very pretty lady, he thought, but very upset. His concern showed on his face. 'Okay, ma'am. As long as you are alright. If there is anything we can do, please let us know.'
The light went out in the motel room. The man emerged. He checked the door to make sure it was locked.

A large explosion shattered the

peace of the darkness. The blast could be heard kilometres away. It had come from the vicinity of Jargodin's dug-out. The people at the drive-in, Coober Pedy's main source of entertainment, lost interest in the picture. They all wondered what the hell had happened. Their thoughts stayed with them throughout the movie. Some of the cars, whose owners lived in the direction of the blast hastily left.

The explosion had come from Jargodin's place. Neighbours rushed to the scene. The police were there in a few minutes. Nothing prepared them for the macabre sights as their torches probed the darkness.

At first it was hard to find the damage. The dug-out seemed to be intact. The detonation must have been outside and in the front. Debris lay scattered about and a drum twisted out of shape was near the door. The outside wall of the dug-out appeared to be peppered by foreign matter.

On closer inspection, the horror of it all became evident. Bits of flesh, human flesh, some of it with pieces of clothing and bone attached, had been blasted into the sandstone.

As they spread their search in a

widening circle, pieces of mangled flesh and bone were found lying about. One of Jargodin's shoes ripped and blood stained still held the remnants of a foot. Some people were heard to be vomiting in the darkness as they stunmbled across their grisly find.
White-faced with shock, people stood about shaking their heads in disbelief. Paula and Josef were quickly on the scene. As pieces of the body were brought forward to be placed in a bag, Paula's screams could be heard by the shocked bystanders. On the advice of the police Josef took her to the hospital. There she would be given a sedative.

Jargodin's blood stained cap was found by one of the searchers. He came forward, holding it out in front of him and carefully laid it on the ground beside the body bag. The people stared at it in silence. Some blessed themselves.

As the picture emerged, it became evident that Jargodin had been blown to pieces. Jargodin was dead. The Moonlighter was dead.

The news spread in epidemic proportions. As it spread, so did the rumours. The Greeks, the Macedonians, the Serbians, had killed him.

Not one whole piece of his body was found...chunks and bits and pieces. Josef was called upon. He was able to identify scraps of clothing and Jargodin's shoes and cap. He asked to retain his cap. The request was granted. The police found a letter on the table in Jargodin's dug-out. It was in his hand-writing. It was a suicide note. They were satisfied.

Small groups gathered at various points around the town. Talking was hush-toned. Ruffoes was packed with Jargodin's friends and countrymen. The atmosphere was of utter dis-belief. The Greeks, Macedonians and Serbians were conspicuous by their absence...It was safer at home. A lot of Jargodin's friends were angry.

Josef made a brief appearance at the restaurant. He talked earnestly with a few friends the went over to Nick. 'Josef, what can I say?' Nick said as Josef approached.

'Nothing Nick. If anyone asks, the funeral will be at three o'clock tomorrow afternoon. We will bury what we have of him.' He shuddered. He put his hand in his pocket and took out a roll of notes. He peeled off two hundred dollars. 'Give the boys a drink Nick.

Don't let them do anything foolish.'

Nick pushed Josef's hand aside. 'The drinks are on me tonight Josef. He was a good friend of mine too. Ah, shit, what he have to do that for?' The tears came to Nick's eyes.

'Thanks Nick. I have to go now. Johnny is looking after Paula. I will see you later.' Toasts were drunk repeatedly...Tales of his escapades were told over and over. In Coober Pedy they became folk lore.

'Jargodin, The Moonlighter.'

BOOK 2

CHAPTER..1.

I was sitting at my kitchen table when the blast shattered the silence. 'Holy bloody hell,' I muttered. 'What the hell was that?' I had a strong sense of unease. It was not long after dark. I had eaten and done the necessary cleaning up chores.

I lived on the outskirts of town and the explosion had come from the other end of the fringe. Down Jargodin's way, I thought. It had to be quite a few sticks of gelegnite...maybe a drum of petrol...perhaps a porta gas bottle...It worried me. I tried to concentrate on the book I was reading, all to no avail...I threw the book down in disgust and decided on a cup of coffee.

The sound of a motor made me look up. Car lights were coming up my entrance. The car stopped outside my door. I recognised Lovro as he got out and came towards me. Somehow I knew...bad news. I walked inside beckoning Lovro to follow.

'You are looking very serious, paisano,' I said. 'Take a seat.' I indicated a chair as I went to get a couple of stubbies from my refrigerator.

Lovro took a sip of beer. 'I have some bad news, Jim...real bad...'

'I can feel it...Give.'

'Jargodin's dead.'

'Holy, shit!' I exclaimed...It dawned on me..'The explosion?' He nodded.

'Oh, Jesus...Oh no'...I shook my head. 'Oh, good Christ no...' I didn't know what to think. In a calm flat voice he told me everything. I, like everybody else was stunned. How long Lovro stayed I don't know. I kept going to the 'frig for another stubbie. I was confused and shattered. I cursed the waste...the stupidity of it all. A small crowd attended the service at Boot Hill. I felt sick in the guts standing there listening to the police Sergeant read the sermon. It all seemed such a cruel stroke of fate as we stood there on that barren, dusty, heartless plateau, a few miles out of town.

Paula, heavily veiled and sobbing quietly, stood, head bowed, between Johnny Dundavic and Josef. It all felt so obscene and foreign to the script of decency...a mockery on life...a couple of plastic bags of flesh and bone being sanctified under the masquerade of religion.

The Sergeant had finished the sermon. The men handling the ropes to lower the bare coffin took up their positions. There were no wreaths as Coober Pedy, a town where you had to buy your water, was bereft of flowers. Just then, Josef walked forward. I saw his hand go into his pocket. The next thing I knew, he had placed Jargodin's cap on top of the coffin. The effect was electric. 'Jesus,' I said to myself. I heard someone behind me say, 'Christ Almighty.' There were gasps and mutters. The men on the ropes seemed to be shocked into a pause in their mission. All eyes were riveted on the cap as it slowly disappeared from view. I felt like vomiting. Somehow it was so macabre and menacing. Everyone was affected by the act. It was the punch that flattened us all.

The crowd dispersed in silence. I made my way over to Paula, Johnny and Josef who were last to leave. I had been accepted into their close circle of friendship...One of the family. I shook hands with Josef and Johnny and gave Paula a warm hug as I kissed her veiled cheek. Words were unnecessary...They would also have been inadequate.

Johnny took me aside. 'Jim, we need

your help...'

'Yes, sure, anything I can do Johnny, I will. You know that.'

'Paula and I are going straight to the airport. I have a small plane waiting there. I'm taking Paula to Adelaide to sort out things. Josef will take care of the dug-out and anything necessary this end.' I nodded.

'I have a lot of opal belonging to Jargodin and Paula. I don't want to sell here on the field. I want you to come down to Adelaide tomorrow. Can you manage that?'

'Well, I guess so.' I frowned. 'You don't need me down there Johnny to sell some opal. Hell, you have all the contacts you need.'

He could see my concern. 'No, there is something else. Incidentally, you will be well paid.' He grabbed my arm and spoke quietly and earnestly. 'Jim, trust me. I need you in Adelaide. Can you come tomorrow?'

By his tone, I realised he was serious. I didn't hesitate.

'Consider it done. I'll be there tomorrow.'

'Good. I'll meet your plane. Have you got enough money to come down?'

I nodded. 'Yes, that will be okay.'

'Now, not a word to anyone. Don't tell a soul where you are going or that you are going...Okay?

Once again I nodded. What the hell was this all about?

'Josef will be around your place later to see you. I'd best go.' We shook hands.

I was last out of the cemetry. As I was about to get into my car, I looked back. In my mind I had a clear picture of Jargodin's laughing face. I looked at the desolate forbiding place where his remains lay. I looked up at the sky...Jesus, I thought, if there is an after life, it has to be a better joint than this. I drove slowly back to town, my mind a jumble of thoughts and regrets. That bloody cap haunted me. I went down to the Tin shed and picked up a carton of stubbies. Inside the shed, people sat around in small huddles. Everyone was subdued, yet there was a feeling of anger in the air.

The aborigines were conspicuous by their silence. They sat in quiet groups which was most unusual. Jargodin was a good friend to them. I had the feeling that if anyone had said anything against Jargodin, the place would have erupted. I went back to my dug-out.

Josef arrived soon after. He handed me a thousand dollars.

'What the hell is this?'

'Expenses. Johnny insists you take it. He said to tell you, that they are depending on you to be there tomorrow. It is important.'

'Jesus,' I said. 'What is going on.'

CHAPTER.."2.

Sitting before my dug-out beneath the diamond studded sky, I reflected on the past months. My mind flashed back to my first meeting with Jargodin. I had only been on the field for a short period. Like all newcomers, I listened in amazement to all the tall tales. I had stepped into a different world...a world so isolated and fascinating. When anyone talked about the various characters and happenings, they had in me, a receptive listener.

The rebel, the outcast, the adventurer, had always attracted me. The town had been built on the efforts of such people. Some would stay for life, some just passed through; some made fortunes and left for good; some made fortunes, left for the bright lights and returned broke, hoping to make it again.

There was no television in Coober Pedy at the time. It seemed to me, the afternoon and evening gossip around the hotel and drinking venues, featured Jargodin and his exploits, real or imaginary. It was like a never ending saga...The Blue Hills of Coober Pedy.

The hotel had been burnt down and

trading had carried on down a lane beside the B.P., in what was affectionately known as 'The Tin Shed.' I was sitting at one of the badly scarred tables one afternoon deep in thought. I nursed a near empty stubbie.

'Ah, my friend, you are miles away. Good thoughts I hope.' Shaken out of my train of thought, I looked up. There was no mistaking the speaker. Open necked shirt, double breasted coat buttoned over, cap squarely on his head, engaging wide grin and piercing black eyes that danced with amusement...Jargodin...I grinned back.

'You have just broken into some very private thoughts...That will cost you a beer.' I drank the rest of my stubbie and handed him the empty. He laughed, touched his cap in salutation and gave a slight bow.

'My pleasure,' he said. So started a rare and fascinating friendship. The guy intrigued me.

One evening, unexpectedly, he arrived at my dug-out with half a dozen stubbies. As he entered, I watched his gaze slowly take in my living quarters. Like a lot of these underground accomodations, mine was one large room; about fifteen metres long and seven metres wide. I like to keep a reasonably tight ship and I saw the nod of approval as he noted the orderliness and cleanliness of my camp.

I had schooled myself into keeping typed notes of events that happened on the field, with the hope that someday I might use them. His arrival coincided with my gathering of papers and closing my portable typewriter.

'Mmm,' he said. 'you are a writer?'

'Not exactly,' I laughed, 'but, yes I do write and jot down notes.' I shrugged. 'Who knows? One day I may get lucky and get something published.'

'Ah, ha! My name is in there?' He pointed to the papers.

'You egotistical bastard,' I thought. I looked at him for a few seconds then nodded. 'Yes, your name is in there.'

'That is good. Maybe when we get to know each other better, I will give you plenty to write about.'

'I am sure you could,' I answered dryly. We both laughed.

It became a habit for Jargodin to drop in for a drink and a yarn. He would often bring Paula. I then became one of the few people invited around to their dug-out for a meal. My camp, like most others, was never locked. Often I would come home to find a note on my kitchen table ....Come around for a meal, Paula...I never refused.

I learnt their full story...They trusted me. They were a fascinating couple...Never have I seen two people so suited and attuned to each other. They were like a tandem bicycle...take one of the riders away and the scene was not complete.

I was on the side-lines...a spectator...I couldn't judge, as I had never walked a mile in their shoes.

'You have enough money, Jargodin. Give it away. One day, some bastard will blow your brains out.'

He would just laugh. 'I'm not ready yet,' would be the reply.

Paula would shrug with the resignation of her race. 'I pray,' was her response.

I saw Jargodin after Paula was lured away. I knew the full story. Johnny Dondovic came up occasionally and we became firm friends. He would often stay with me. We would sit talking into the small hours of the morning. I was amazed at his interests and his influence. His 'semi-legit,' espresso bar was but a front.

'If it wasn't the Mafia, there would be no problem. Those bastards are hard to beat. Hard to beat but it is still possible to do so. The part that worries me is, if we don't act soon, it will be too late.'

Johnnies words came back to me.
News of Paula's return quickly spread. Lovro had come around to my dug-out to let me know. 'I'd say they will be pulling out in a hurry. They seem to think that someone looking for revenge will follow.'

I nodded. 'That is for sure,' I replied.

'I've got a message from Johnny for you. He said to stay put. Don't try and contact Jargodin or him, as he will be in touch.'

I frowned wondering what was going on; but knowing Johnny had his reasons, I accepted the fact.

All this and more tumbled through my mind. I shook myself out of my reverie. I had to prepare for tomorrow's flight.

CHAPTER. 3.

Johnny met me at the airport. He had me booked in at a nearby motel. I was waiting for him to enlighten me.
'Jim, don't ask me any questions. You will know all in good time. I'm going to drop you off at the motel and be ready to be picked up at eight tomorrow morning. Don't check out. The room has been paid for a week.'
I was puzzled. He laughed. 'Look, my friend, everything is okay. I'll tell you tomorrow. They have T.V., here. Something you don't have in Coober, so get in front of the idiot box and relax. I'll be here at eight.' We shook hands and Johnny left. I was more confused than ever. The television, being a novelty, helped pass the hours but I still had a feeling of unease. there was something missing. My thoughts kept floating back to Paula and Jargodin. I could still see that God forsaken, barren cemetry. I could see that cap. That last scene was vivid in my mind.
It was good to be back in civilisation once again. Nice comfortable room, hot water that gushed with pressure out of a

shower. Nice not to worry about how much water you were using. It was good to sit in a clean restaurant and order a meal, cooked, served and presented with class. It helped ease the pain. I had ordered an early breakfast. I was showered and dressed in decent casual clothes and reading the Adelaide Advertiser, when the knock came on the door. I had already undone the safety latch.

'Come in, Johnny. It's unlocked.' I stood up.

Johnny, his face lit up and eyes sparkling, opened the door and stood aside.

Paula and Jargodin walked in....

I must have looked like a village idiot, standing there. To say I was stunned would be putting it mildly. I never swear in front of women, but I couldn't help myself. 'What the fucking hell is going on?' I half screamed. Only for the fact of Johnny being there giving reality, I think I might have passed out. I was shocked. Was this real, am I dreaming? I looked around. It was all too much. 'Oh, shit, am I going out of my mind?'

The next few minutes...I can't recall. There were handshakes, kisses, laughter. 'Who the bloody hell did we bury out there?'

Johnny laughed. 'Sit down Jim. I'll tell you everything. Here,' he went to the sideboard. There was a bottle of whisky there. He poured me half a glass of scotch and added a bit of water. 'Drink this. You will probably need it.'

'I need it man! I need it!' I took the glass out of his hand. Johnny told it as it happened.

'So you see, there will be a lot of confusion their end. They haven't a clue what has happened. Everyone believes that Jargodin is buried out there in Boot Hill. The paisanoes will think that Jargodin's mates have knocked Lou and Sergio off and buried them somewhere out on the field. Poor Lou, he never thought he would end up in Boot Hill. Sergio will leave town and he won't be game to talk. They will put the ladders down today after I ring Josef. Paula and Jargodin are booked on an overseas flight in an hours time. One day when all is settled down they can return.

'Meantime, I will tell Bruno, Paula has gone into hiding, but that she is quite okay. I will tell him enough to put his mind at ease. Her father will cop some flak. That can't be helped.

He'll get over it.. He will lose prestige and power. The big boys will have more important things to worry about.' Johnny shrugged. 'We beat the bastards,' Johnny said.

I listened in amazement.

Jargodin walked outside and returned carrying a box. He must have left it outside the door before he came in. He handed it to me.

'For you Jim, from Paula and I.' He nodded. 'Open it.'

I was still trying to comes to terms with it all. I opened the box. A brand new Remington portable typewriter stared at me. I lifted the cover. There was a bundle of hundred dollar bills on the keyboard. $5,000.

I looked up at them. 'I can't accept this....'

'Before you go any further,' Jargodin said, 'Just listen. Paula and I have plenty. That money means little to us, besides,' he grinned, 'it was given to me.'

'Oh, shit,' I laughed.

'That five grand gets you writing. I want you to tell our story. If you like, let's have an agreement. That money gives me five percent. How's that?'

I shook my head. Everything was

happening so fast. I laughed. 'You have yourself a deal.' We shook hands.

'Right, Jim. You promise me, you will tell the world.'

I nodded. 'I promise.'

I looked at Paula. She looked beautiful. She was radiant. She smiled and came over to me. She kissed me on the cheek. 'Your friendship has meant a lot to us Jim,' then in mock severity, she said, 'you write that bloody book.'

I laughed. 'I promise...I promise.' There was now a feeling of euphoria among us. We were on a high. Johnny brought us back to earth. 'There is a 'plane to be caught,' he said as he looked at his watch.

Jargodin walked over to the wall mirror. He took a something out of his pocket. A few seconds later he turned around. We all chuckled. The transformation was amazing. He now wore a neatly trimmed beard. He put on a pair of sun-glasses and a bloody new cap.

'How's that?' he asked. 'I seem to have misplaced my old cap.'

I groaned. 'Oh, no, that cap. I had nightmares over it.'

'It was a bit dramatic,' Johnny said wryly.

I shook my head. 'It sure was. Do you mind if I change the subject. 'That beard suits you.' We all laughed.

'No-one would ever know you Jargodin. We don't want somebody recognising you before you get on the 'plane,' Johnny said.

Paula was wearing a cute little hat with a veil that came over her eyes. She too put her sunglasses on. Simple little things that made all the difference.

There was a small fenced in area on the concourse which allowed visitors to watch all flights. Johnny and I stood there with a bit of apprehension. The finale was yet to be played. Passengers were already streaming across the tarmac to the awaiting 'plane.

The last call for passengers came over the intercom. It seemed all were on board. A man and woman came through the doors and hastily made their way across to the stairs... Paula and Jargodin.. The air hostess at the bottom of the stairs looked at the tickets Paula handed her. She nodded, pointed and gave directions. Paula turned, waved and trotted up the steps.

Jargodin looked in our direction. To

the amazement of the air-hostess, he did the splits, zipped up, bowed to us and ran up the steps to disappear inside.

'The bastard,' Johnny said.

'A showman to the end,' I laughed.

Johnny and I stood shoulder to shoulder as the giant machine rumbled to life and started its stately roll down the runway. We watched as it turned, angrily roared to power, careered along the tarmac then took it's majestic path into the heavens. We waited until it disappeared from view.

'I have a book to write,' I muttered to myself.

The bewitching hour...a full moon flooded the silent semi-desert landscape........